The Plight
Before
Christmas

The Plight Before Christmas

A Collection of Captivating Stories
By North Texas Christian Writers

The Plight Before Christmas
A Collection of Captivating Stories
By North Texas Christian Writers
With Frank Ball

Second Printing: October 2012

ISBN 13: 978-0615684178
ISBN 10: 0615684173

http://www.NTChristianWriters.com

Published by:
North Texas Christian Writers
P.O. Box 820802
Fort Worth, TX 76182

Special Thanks

To the Writing Coaches,

Writer's Group Leaders,

Story Contributors,

And Other Supporters

Of North Texas Christian Writers

The Christian Writer's Prayer

Heavenly Father, let every expression from my heart bring honor to your name. As it is in heaven, have your way in my life, so I can complete the work you have assigned to me.

Today, give me the right words to say. Forgive my narrow-mindedness as I seek to help others. If I am tempted to let other desires consume my time, deliver me from the evil that prevents my picking up the pen and releasing the burden of my soul.

You are my King, possessor of all ability and wisdom. If I should write any worthwhile words, they will be from you, and always for your glory.

Amen.

– Frank Ball

Foreword
by Jan Brand

Many people have wonderful memories of Christmas spent with family and friends, celebrating the most important event in history—the birth of the Son of God, the Savior of the world.

Some children dream of "sugar plums" as they anticipate opening brightly covered packages, but others feel the pain and loneliness of having no one with them to share the occasion.

Our joys are not always without pain, and the *plight* often precedes the *prize*. Whether pain or pleasure, the season stirs hope within us because God's Son came to proclaim peace on earth, goodwill toward men.

This book is filled with stories that will warm your heart while making you laugh or cry. Sometimes both. Some are true, others are fiction, but all of them show God's care for us—wherever we are, whoever we are, whatever the circumstance.

Our King of kings and Lord of lords, the Prince of Peace has come, and we need never be alone again. Because of the Babe in Bethlehem, we can belong to the family of God. I invite you to follow the emotional journeys in each story and experience the love of Christ in action.

To know him is to love him.

Table of Contents

Six Weeks Till the Deadline
by Frank Ball

Twas six weeks till the deadline, when all through the house,
My computer was working with help from my mouse.
The due date was taped to the screen's top with care,
In hopes a bestseller would rise below there.

The elves were all settled down snugly in bed,
While thoughts of acceptance still danced in my head.
My words in a turmoil, my hands in my lap,
I rested my eyes for a nice little nap.

When out on the snow there arose such a clatter,
I looked from my desk to see what was the matter.
I took to the keyboard, both hands in a flash,
My fingers were wanting a super good smash.

The moon on the slopes of the new-fallen snow
Gave light to great scenes but the plot wouldn't go.
Then what to my wondering mind should appear:
A wonderful plan for my story made clear.

Just a little suspense, oh, so lively and quick,
And I knew the right twist that would make a neat trick.
More lofty than eagles, great phrases they came,
I whistled and shouted and dreamed of my fame!

No blunders. Go writer! Now throw in the colon.
On, comma! On, period! On, em-dash and question!
To the best of the books! To the top of the wall!
Time to dash away! Dash away! Dash away all!

As the leaves that before the wild hurricane fly,
So the characters' obstacles clashed and they cried.
Going on with my story, the chapters they flew,
All the kids would be pleased and the dads would be too.

But then, in a twinkling, I thought about SCOOP.
In plotting and writing I had to regroup.
Situation and Character had to be right,
The Objective and Obstacle followed by Plight.

Needing title and plot that would captivate well,
I sought expert advice that would help me excel.
The elves had no skill to say what would work best,
But help from my writer's group calmed my unrest.

Their eyes how they twinkled. Their thoughts were so merry!
Improving my story, they made me feel cheery.
For each little book would be wrapped with a bow,
And parents and children would shout "ho-ho-ho."

As I looked for a way to print millions of books
All the agents and editors gave me sad looks.
No printer could do the amount I was needing.
I ran out of breath while relentlessly pleading.

With his presses so fast, a right jolly old elf
Quickly claimed he could print them but not by himself.
A wink of his eye and a twist of his head,
Soon gave me to know I had nothing to dread.

With hardly a word, he went straight to design,
Creating a cover that looked really fine.
And laying the wording across every page,
The copy was good, every chapter a rage.

I sprang to my sleigh with my bag of bestsellers
And knew what to say as a help for all writers
"Your success won't be easy," I cried through the night,
"But your Christmas is best when you make time to write."

Tree-Topper
by LaWanda Bailey

While driving to the Christmas tree lot, Caroline wondered how she would fill the void left by her divorce. Her young son and daughter missed their father, a fact that became more obvious as they kept searching for the perfect tree. At the third stop, the kids found an eight-foot Scotch pine they said was just right. With credit card in hand, she paid the salesman and thanked him for tying the tree to the roof of their car.

At home, the kids tried to help, but Caroline supplied the muscle to untie the tree, drag it into the living room, and wrestle it into the stand. Reluctantly, she drooped stockings from the mantle, dangled stars from the ceiling, and nestled wrapped gifts beneath the tree. While she added the lights, the kids hung ornaments as high as they could reach. Two shiny balls fell to the floor and broke, a fitting reminder of what this Christmas would be like.

Weekends dragged on, and work on Mondays brought welcome relief. Her children needed twice as much of her, and she had half as much to give. Her

4

single income paid double bills. She ached with the newness of her shaken life, lying in jagged pieces, shattered like a glass nativity scene dropped on the floor.

On Christmas Eve, Caroline dressed her youngsters in party clothes and reluctantly handed them over like wrapped gifts to spend the night with their father. *How can I celebrate Christmas without my kids?* she thought. *With my luck, even Santa won't stop by.*

In the empty house, strains of "Have Yourself a Merry Little Christmas" tweaked her last nerve, and she threw her fuzzy house slippers at the television screen. Divorce had flipped her world upside-down. She preferred root canals over Christmas festivities.

Caroline didn't have to spend her holiday alone. It was her choice. She had turned down every party invitation. No more goodwill and holiday smiles, perfect couples, and Christmas carols. She would wallow in her mud-pit of misery, cry till her eyes puffed, and if the mood hit her, scream like Jamie Lee Curtis in *Halloween*.

Curled up on the carpet beside the tree, she watched the Christmas lights blink in rhythm to "jingle bells, jingle bells" playing on the television.

This is too much merriment.

With a kick, she turned off the television.

She breathed in the evergreen scent and exhaled the words: "Help me, Jesus." It was just a simple prayer, recognizing her need, not with any expectation for an answer.

Up through the branches, she saw something wedged between a branch and the trunk. High, close to the top. What was it? Why hadn't she noticed it before?

Caroline reached into the prickly limbs and removed a perfectly formed nest, no bigger than a teacup. Threadlike strands lay woven tightly against one other, and the inside was scooped into a cozy haven.

She cradled the nest in her hands, imagining the mother bird and her wide-mouthed offspring. There in the woods, storms must have thrashed their fragile shelter, but it had survived. She thought about hungry hawks perching nearby, while the cheeping infants were safely in their mother's care. After the fledglings had flown away, woodsmen came with chain saws. When the tree crashed to the ground, the branches still held the nest securely. Even when the flatbed truck bounced along uneven roads, the nest hadn't fallen. The day she drove home with the tree, the wind whipped the branches with near-hurricane force. Nature and humans assailed the nest from every side, yet it remained safe, hidden in its secure resting place in the arms of the tree. Why couldn't her house have been this strong, instead of being torn apart by divorce?

After placing the woven shelter back into the treetop, she retrieved her house slippers and sniffled her way to the bedroom. Sprawled facedown across the bed, she pounded the mattress with her fists. Tears soaked through the patchwork quilt.

"Our honeymoon quilt," she said, wishing for the joy that was forever lost. Tears gave way to moans as she rolled over, seized a pillow, and punched it into submission.

Deep from within, emotions swelled, geysers of anger and despair surging upward. She sat up and tried to catch her breath, but a need for oxygen was no match for the eruption of suppressed emotions. When she opened her mouth to take a breath, the pain burst through the surface of her un-grieved loss. Groans gushed upward, one after the other, each one stronger than the last. From the depth of her soul, grief pushed up and out, her voice wailing in a resonance unfamiliar to her. Afraid that the *Halloween* scream was on its way, she buried her face in the pillow.

In the next instant, she envisioned the brave mother bird, wings spread over her little ones while thunder roared and rains pelted the nest.

Caroline's failures as a mother and a wife, her ex's failures as a father and husband—none of that could shake the security of nesting in God's hands. Forget the fears, the loneliness, and the creditors. She might be exhausted and discouraged, but she didn't have to be defeated. When her children came home, their nest would provide them the warmth and comfort they needed. Nothing could destroy their safe haven.

After slipping into her fuzzy slippers, Caroline went to the closet and pulled out her red satin dress. Caroline took a deep breath, then another. She dabbed a tissue at her eyes.

Okay, I'll rethink my circumstances. I can't be outdone by a tiny bird.

She thought of her own nest where she and her young ones rested in God's powerful arms.

Surely God's arms were stronger than the branches of a Scotch pine.

Peace on Earth
by R.W. Ley

Just past midnight, Sergeant Sheldon led his small patrol past the shattered brick walls of what had once been a suburban neighborhood. This area of Chicago had been hit hard in the recent bombing and was now classified a "no-civilian zone."

"Wait," Sergeant Sheldon whispered. Had it not been for the smell of wood smoke drifting on the chilled breeze, he might have missed the faint glow from the second house on the right. He didn't want to lead his men into a trap.

With his AR-52 at the ready position, he flipped up his night-vision goggles, knowing that a campfire would blind him when they burst inside. With two fingers, he instructed Shimwa and McCallum to move left, Jones and Hernandez to the right. Private Stokes stayed on his flank. As quietly as icy ground and loose rubble allowed, they worked through the debris and approached the building on three sides.

The door splintered at the impact of his boot. He stepped inside, his rifle pointed at whatever was huddling in the shadows. Stokes entered on his left, rifle ready.

A woman, wrapped in the remains of an old blanket, jumped up from the fire.

"Freeze." Sheldon knew the danger of female rebel soldiers who dressed as civilians. "Don't even think of reaching for anything." He whistled in three successive chirps. Shimwa stepped over the broken window sill, Hernandez through a gap in the wall. Jones and McCallum remained outside.

"We've done nothing wrong." She let the blanket fall so he could she wasn't armed.

"You're in a no-civilian zone. That's enough. Who are you?"

"My name is Katrin. This is my son, Michael. He can't hear you. He's been deaf since he was two. My sister, Marta, is over there. She's sick."

"What're you doing here?" When she didn't answer, Sheldon walked to several bundles stacked near the fire and kicked at them. "Stokes, check these packs. See what they're carrying."

Katrin made a move toward the packs.

Sheldon chambered a round. The metallic clang stopped her. "I wouldn't do that, lady."

She stepped back toward her sister, who groaned and appeared to be in pain.

Stokes opened the first three bundles—just clothes and personal items. He untied the canvas duffle bag and turned it upside down.

"Hey Sarge, look at this." Brightly wrapped boxes fell onto the floor.

Marta moaned as she pushed up on one elbow. "Those are for the baby." She groaned again, this time in obviously intense pain.

Katrin rushed to her sister's side. "The baby is coming now?" She pushed the hair off her sister's face.

Marta nodded and fell back again.

"Shimwa," Sheldon said, "get over here and see to her. Didn't they send you to first-aid training?"

Shimwa jumped without hesitation. "Yeah, but all they covered was bullet holes, broken bones, and hang-nails. Don't we need to boil water or something?"

Sheldon muttered a curse. "McCallum! You and Jones get in here." With a few terse words, he outlined the situation.

McCallum loosened the lid on his canteen and placed it on the hot coals. "It ain't much, but it's all we got."

Katrin signed something to her son, who nodded and pulled a blanket from one of the clothes packs.

"Jones, take Stokes and bring up the Jeep. We'll need to transport these people to the detention center in the morning."

"We won't go," Katrin said, seated at her sister's side. "We've done nothing wrong."

Sheldon kicked at one of the wrapped boxes. The shiny green paper was imprinted with nativity scenes. "Possession of contraband is enough. Christmas has been outlawed or haven't you heard that?"

Marta's scream cut off Katrin's answer and expressed the greater truth. All that was important was giving birth.

Katrin knelt and pushed the presents back into the bag. "They aren't contraband, as you call it. They're simply gifts for the baby."

"They are what I say they are. Now go tend to

10

your sister."

Shimwa gave Katrin a grim look. "It won't be long. I don't know how to judge these things, but I think your sister's having trouble."

Katrin muttered under her breath, eyes closed.

Sheldon moved closer. "Lady, are you asking for more trouble? What do you think you're doing, praying?"

She kept mumbling, as if she hadn't heard him. When she opened her eyes, she showed no fear. "Prove it."

Marta's screams brought everyone's attention to the fireside. This would not be an easy delivery. The night wore on and Marta appeared weaker as she labored to deliver her child. Shimwa and Katrin stayed beside her.

From outside, just before dawn, Sheldon heard an infant cry.

"It's a boy." Shimwa's announcement included a tone of panic. "The mother needs medical help," she whispered. "We need to get her to Medvac, not the detention center."

Jones called from the Jeep. "Sarge, HQ's on the horn. They're recalling all patrols." He looked at Sheldon. "They said don't bring in collaterals and don't leave 'em behind."

"You're sure you got the message straight?"

"Yeah, Sarge, I'm sure."

Sheldon cursed again. "Confirm delivery of the message. Shimwa, McCallum, move out. Load up while I take care of matters here."

"What are you going to do?" Shimwa looked toward the house.

"Follow orders. Now get to the Jeep. Now!"

"Sarge…" She broke off at Sheldon's harsh stare. "Got it."

The five soldiers were climbing into the Jeep when four sharp rifle retorts sounded from inside. Jones and McCallum were about to head back in when Sergeant Sheldon came out of the house. "Okay, move out."

Five pairs of eyes looked at their Sergeant in shock.

"You didn't—" Shimwa's words were cut off by the muffled sound of an infant crying.

Sheldon climbed in beside Hernandez. "I said, move out."

Jones glanced at his Sergeant. "How should the report read?"

"Did you hear the shots?"

"Yes."

"Did you see any survivors?"

"I heard—"

"That's not what I asked you, corporal. Did you *see* any collaterals left behind?"

"No, sarge, I didn't see any collaterals left behind."

"That's what the report should say. Also report the loss of my pack. I'll have to get a new one from supply."

Shimwa sat in front of Sheldon, watching over his shoulder as they drove past the dilapidated house.

Sheldon watched her closely, noting silently when her eyes widened. A suggestion of a smile twitched her lip. She leaned forward and whispered, "Peace on earth, Sarge."

Sheldon grunted and kept his eyes focused hard ahead.

Christmas Medicine
by John Savell

"Have you finished your Christmas story?" My writer's group leader asked.

I cringed at his reminder of the deadline and mumbled that I'd been too busy with my current book. "Maybe I can write something by next month." I'm sure he saw through my lack of enthusiasm. The last thing I wanted to do was write a Christmas story.

Driving home, I struggled over why I wasn't interested in writing something Christmasy. Everyone else in my group was excited about submitting their stories. My lack of inspiration seemed especially odd, given that Christmas was my favorite time of year.

Then it hit me.

This would be my first Christmas without Mom. Never again would her face light up when I walked through the door with goodies to put under the tree. I'd never hear the special way she said "hello" or "I love you." I'd never hug her neck or hold her hand.

Tears welled up in my eyes.

Life had felt empty since Mom passed away after a

six-year battle with a rare form of cancer. Why did it have to be rare? Why couldn't it have been common and easily treated?

I remembered the day Mom called. "John," she said in a solemn tone. " I have something to tell you. I have cancer."

Her words left me numb. This can't be happening to my mom, not her. After the initial shock, I asked about treatment.

"I'm having surgery in two weeks. Medicine will take care of the rest."

I relaxed knowing they had medicine for Mom. Her physician was world-renowned, and so was the hospital.

The surgeon removed ten malignant tumors. Two others were inoperable. That was okay. Mom said the medicine would take care of the rest.

Mom's health improved for a while. Then the news came. The cancer was growing at a faster rate. Her physician suggested another medicine normally used on a different type of cancer. Mom agreed. Our family prepared for a second round of chemo, hopeful this new medicine would work.

It didn't.

It only made her worse. She lost her hair and spent most days throwing up and struggling to find a comfortable position in her favorite chair. Her appetite disappeared, and restful sleep became a distant memory.

I never felt so helpless. I spent hours on the Internet and talking with physician friends in hope of finding what medicine might rid her body of the cancer, but found nothing. If I had studied medicine in school instead of psychology, I might have discovered a cure.

14

In six years, Mom went through five rounds of chemotherapy. I don't know how she survived. Though her body broke down under the onslaught of the chemo, her spirit never wavered. Her laughter always filled the room, whether at home or in the hospital. At times, I felt angry with the medicine that was supposed to heal her, frustrated that it made her sick instead.

Mom would pat my hand and say, "John, it's going to be okay. Whether God heals me or I go on home, it will be all right." Despite fighting the greatest battle of her life, she shared her heart with everyone. The hospital staff loved her. Even when vomiting into a bucket at the side of her bed, she never lost the twinkle in her eyes.

During the last round of chemo, her physician suggested an experimental drug that showed promise in preliminary studies. She'd be part of a trial group to determine if the FDA would approve the medicine. I didn't want Mom to be a guinea pig for some drug company's experiment. After four rounds of failed chemo, I wanted her to say no, believing this medicine would also fail, but Mom agreed to the study.

A month later, Mom had a PET scan to see if the drug helped. To everyone's surprise, the cancer had shrunk, not a lot, but enough to know the medicine had a positive effect. Finally, we'd found the right drug to heal Mom. We celebrated. The worst was over. She'd get through this. It might take a while for her to regain her strength, but it was just a matter of time until she returned to the things she loved most—shopping with my sisters, spending time with her grandchildren, and entertaining a house full of family and friends.

After another month, we knew something was

wrong. She wasn't getting better. Though the tumors had shrunk, they hadn't gone away. In fact, the cancer had spread to other areas, requiring surgery to remove part of her intestines. She remained in a semi-conscious state for weeks.

When she finally woke, her physician said he could do nothing more. He had no more medicine for her. All he could do was make her comfortable. After a referral to hospice, he sent her home to die.

I struggled with the thought of Mom not being with me much longer. She was the heart of our family. I couldn't imagine a world without her. I felt like a failure for not finding the right medicine to cure her.

As I exited the freeway, I relived my helplessness in those six years. Tears filled my eyes, blurring my vision, flowing down my cheeks. "Mom, I'm sorry the treatment didn't work. I'm sorry we didn't find the right medicine. I wish I'd had medicine for you."

As if God saw my tears, a small voice said, *But you did. Not only did you find the right medicine, but you gave her just what she needed.*

I wiped the tears from my cheeks. "What do you mean?"

During those difficult days, you gave your mom the medicine of your Time. When you drove seven hours on weekends to visit, you gave her the medicine she needed most. Your phone calls each week encouraged and lifted her spirits.

I checked the rearview mirror, reassuring myself that I was alone in my car. The voice continued.

Second, you gave her the medicine of your Tenderness. Remember the times she poured out her heart during the darkest moments? You listened attentively to the same stories over and over. Your patience soothed her spirit. And there were the times

16

you rubbed lotion on feet racked with pain from the chemo.

I swallowed hard.

And last, you gave her the medicine of your Love, to let her know she was not alone, that someone walked alongside her each step of the way.

I again brushed my tears aside.

And one more thing.

I listened intently.

When you hold My hand, know that I'm holding hers.

I pulled into my driveway and let those words sink in. My burden of helplessness was lifted. Peace settled over me when I realized I had given Mom exactly what she needed. I gave her the medicine of my Time, Tenderness, and Love.

The medicine I thought would help had failed, and the medicine she needed most, God gave through me and others. Mom also had medicine for me—*peace* to calm my angry storm, *hope* of life beyond the grave, and *love* to let me know I'll never walk alone.

God gave me an early Christmas gift, the gift of knowing I always have medicine to give. And he gave me a Christmas story to write.

This first Christmas will always be special. Mom is now home.

Merry Christmas, Mom, I love you.

Some Assembly Required
by Carol Hatheway Scott

As soon as I heard the car come up the driveway, I opened the front door to welcome Natalie with a big hug. Keeping my five-year-old granddaughter was always a thrill, but it was also a huge challenge. How would I entertain her all day while Mom was shopping, so she would be thrilled and want to keep coming back?

"Merry Christmas, Gramma." She skipped into the living room and ran for the Christmas tree, sparkling with tinsel. Where did she get all that energy? She twirled in a dance and let her soft black curls bounce above her shoulders while enjoying the colored lights and sweet smell of pine. Her eyes glistened when she saw the presents under the tree, with their bright wrapping paper and fancy bows.

Natalie took all of three seconds to find the one she was looking for. "This one's for me, isn't it?" She reached out and lightly tugged on the bow.

"Yes, you're right. That one has your name on it, but we don't touch the presents until Christmas morning."

18

She pulled her hand back, her lower lip sticking out in a pucker, which reminded me of her mother at that age.

A glance toward the coffee table took her in that direction, her eyes fixed on the tray of cookies. "Oh, can I have one, Gramma? Please?" Not daring to reach without permission, she held her hands together.

"Yes, of course."

Her dimples emerged and quickly disappeared as she took a big bite of the candy-sprinkled sugar cookie.

What could we do that she would think was fun? The cookies were already made. All the decorating was done. "Natalie," I asked, "Would you like to help me set up the manger scene while we eat cookies?" Dozens of past assembly times by Natalie's uncles had left the pieces worn, torn, and chipped. Fortunately, I hadn't yet thrown them away.

Natalie nodded, her mouth too full to answer out loud.

She sat next to me on the floor as I smoothed out the white fake-fur ground of the nativity set, which functioned as "snow." As I unwrapped the first piece, I wondered if she would notice how bad it looked.

"Oooh! How pretty," she said, as if each unwrapped piece were another Christmas present for her. "Look, Mary's dress got torn while she rode the donkey all the way to Bethlehem." She pointed to the chipped edges of Mary's blue gown, incorporating the damage into her story of the first Christmas. She placed it exactly to her satisfaction.

While she arranged the cows and donkeys and pre-tended they were munching on the bits of hay, I unwrapped more figures. Two wise men. Where was the third one?

She grabbed another cookie.

I kept searching, but it didn't seem to be here. How could we tell the story without a wise man to bring the third gift to the baby Jesus?

"I'll put Joseph next to the tired donkey." Natalie picked up the figure and put it in place. The "tired donkey," an ear missing and a hoof glued on, had galloped into this scene many times. She handled the donkey gently, as if she knew it needed tender care.

"Does Baby Jesus come next?" She cradled the infant reverently in the curve of her cupped hand. Amazingly, the infant had survived without a chip, perhaps because my boys had held the tiny figure with the same awe.

"Yes, put him in the manger." I pushed the legs of the manger to stand it straight but it slowly reverted to its worn, tilted position.

"It looks like one of the animals stood in his bed doesn't it, Gramma?"

"Maybe, but there wasn't room for Jesus anywhere else."

"Do the wise men come next?" Natalie pointed to the figure wearing a crown, holding a gold vase.

"No, the shepherds were first to hear the angel's announcement."

Gingerly, Natalie gathered the four shepherds and five sheep. While she placed them outside the manger, I frantically searched the bottom of the box for the missing wise man.

Natalie removed the light bulb attached to the top of the stable and handed it to me. "Let's light the star so the wise men can find Baby Jesus."

I plugged the cord into the wall socket. The bulb hung loosely, flickering on and off. It needed to be tightened.

"Oh, look!" Natalie said in an excited tone. "It twinkles."

I squeezed each crumpled tissue to see where the missing wise man was hiding. Nothing. What was I going to do?

"Okay, where's the first wise man and his gift?" she asked. "What did he bring?"

I gave the cracked figure to her. "The wise men brought the best gifts. The Bible mentions gold first."

She placed the matching camel next to the first wise man in the set. "And the next one brought *Frank's incense*, right?"

"Yes, *frankincense*." I smiled, nodded, and handed the second wise man to her.

Natalie lined him up behind the first so they could offer their gifts to Jesus one by one. She took his camel and marched it behind the procession.

After adjusting the wise men and their camels to the positions she wanted, she held out her hand. "And the last one brought perfume that cost a lot."

I shook my head in frustration. "I can't find the other wise man." I showed her my empty hands.

"Uh, oh," Natalie said with a sigh. "Jesus is s'posed to get three gifts."

"I know." I fluffed up the tissues. "I've looked everywhere."

Natalie peered into the empty box.

"I can't find his camel either," I said. I lifted the box and she looked under it.

She looked around the room and stopped when

she spotted her own present under the tree. "Can I give him my present?"

"Yes, that's a wonderful idea."

Natalie's dimples deepened.

"We usually can't touch the presents until Christmas day, but I believe we could make an exception for Jesus."

Natalie picked up her red-and-green package with its golden bow, marched back to the manger scene, and knelt directly behind the second wise man. "Jesus, here is my best present. When I open it on your birthday, I'll remember it's really yours and you're letting me use it."

"Yes, Lord," I said, joining her in prayer, "help us remember everything we have is a gift from you. Jesus is the best gift of all."

Wrapping Up the Scarf
by Anna L. Russell

With her husband, Cliff, beside her, Laura Jordon sat in the OB/GYN waiting room, fanning the pages of an upside-down magazine. She didn't care to look up, since she was the only woman there who didn't have a bulging belly. Whatever it took, she wanted a family.

So she waited, not sure what the tests would reveal.

In the doctor's office, Laura sensed something was wrong before anything was said.

"The tests show significant fibroids and scar tissue on the fallopian tubes," Dr. Granberry said. "I'm sorry, but conception is doubtful."

On the way home, Laura said nothing until they were pulling into the garage. "Cliff," she said, "with our savings we have enough to adopt."

"Let's pray about that." Cliff seemed to be strongly considering it.

A week later, Laura was working with an adoption agency, filling out endless forms, giving references, and answering questions. They had to be "evaluated" to

23

determine if they would be good parents. "Grilled, humiliated, and tortured" was the more accurate description. She would never do this a second time.

After answering yet another question, Laura asked, "Can we adopt more than one child? A brother and sister, maybe?"

Yes, the orphanage in Afghanistan might allow that. The first piece of good news.

Laura waited. Two months went by. More questions. Another form. A financial audit. She kept waiting, about as patiently as a child after Labor Day, who was counting the days until Christmas.

Laura's church was collecting shoeboxes filled with goodies to be sent to poor children overseas, including Afghanistan. Filling the boxes allowed her to dream. With no children to help at home, she could at least be a mom to an orphan somewhere. Into one box, she folded her heavy silk scarf with blue, green, and yellow stripes. It had been handed down for three generations, but she had no child to give it to. Giving it to an orphan who needed a family seemed like the next best thing.

Laura took the small spiral notebook, taped Cliff's photo inside, and tucked it into the folds of the scarf. That way, whoever opened the box could picture having a dad. After adding trinkets and small toys, she squeezed down the lid, fastened it with two thick rubber bands, and wrote *GIRL* on the top.

On Monday morning, two weeks before Christmas, Laura kissed Cliff goodbye, on his way to work, and walked back into an empty house. Too quiet. No kids running down the hallway, screaming.

Seated at the kitchen table, she sipped coffee and

scanned the morning paper. Headline: *Excited Orphans Receive Gifts*. The article described a truckload of shoeboxes distributed to needy kids. The picture showed a girl with arms extended, reaching for her gift.

Laura imagined the girl reaching out to her, felt the joy of their strong embrace, and then realized it was all a dream. When was the adoption agency going to call? Would they ever be approved?

Later that day, she checked the mailbox. A small manila envelope from the agency, with more papers, a DVD, and a note: *Please review the enclosed materials. When you're ready, call me.*

Cliff played the video. Orphans were at play. "There!" he said. "The boy and girl holding hands." He put the video on *pause*.

"What are their names?" Laura touched the screen.

Cliff checked the paperwork. "Fariad and Lala."

"They're beautiful." Laura wasted no time in picking up the phone and calling the agency. "When can we come in?" She put her hand over the receiver, looked at Cliff, and whispered, "Can we be there tomorrow at noon?"

Cliff nodded.

Laura was ready to leave for Bagram the next morning, but she couldn't. More approvals were needed. Passports. Vaccinations. Finally, after another three months, flight reservations.

On the airplane Laura looked down at the clouds. *Lord, would you give us a family? Please cause everything to work out.*

At the orphanage, the director walked Laura and Cliff to a room with a one-way window where they could view the huge room filled with children needing a

25

home. From front to back, left to right, Laura looked at every child but recognized no faces. "Where are Fariad and Lala?" Had someone else already adopted them? Her heart sank. Strange things happen in foreign countries.

"So sorry," the director said in a forceful voice, unusual for a female. "Probably they be with group on playground. I will have them brought."

Something else caught Laura's eye. No, it couldn't be. But the scarf sure looked like the one she had packed in the shoebox. How many blue-green-and-yellow striped scarves could there be?

Laura looked at the director, then turned back to the window. "Who's the tall girl in the far corner, the one with the pretty scarf?"

"That's Anika. She may never be adopted. Too old."

"May I talk to her too?"

In a small room with only a small table and four chairs, Laura and Cliff waited.

Anika came in with the director.

Laura reached toward Anika, but she backed away. "What a lovely scarf. Where did you get it?"

The director translated and gave the explanation to Laura. "Last Christmas, a big truck came, filled with boxes. When she got her box, she removed the rubber straps and found the beautiful scarf inside."

This was too much of a coincidence. She turned to Cliff. "Did you notice Anika's expression when she walked in and saw you? It was like she recognized you."

"We both know that's not possible."

"It might be. Last year when I put together that shoebox, I taped your picture inside a memo pad and put it inside my scarf—and I'd swear this is the same scarf."

"Amazing. Is God trying to tell us something?"

After dismissing Anika, the director came to the table, opened her folder, and looked over the paperwork. "You have the three-year-old boy Fariad and his seventeen-month-old sister Lala. This is correct?"

"Yes," Laura said.

"All is in order, then. You sign, please. Then take them."

"Wait." Cliff stood, as if to protest the arrangement. "What about Anika?" He glanced at Laura, as if seeking her reassurance. He squeezed her hand. "We want Anika too."

"You want the old one? She is eleven years old. Strange you are. I check to see if can arrange."

The following Tuesday, Laura boarded the plane with her new family. Fariad sat on her left, Lala on her right, both with little understanding of where they were or where they were going. Laura didn't understand many Dari words, but as best she could determine, Fariad was fascinated by this house that had wings.

Cliff sat across the aisle, smiling, because Anika was sitting next to him, already so attached to him, she didn't want to let him out of her sight. Anika opened her little notebook, touched the picture, and pointed to Cliff.

All because Laura had wrapped up the scarf.

"That's right," Laura said in broken Dari. "We are a family."

Broken Tradition
by Helmut Knefely

For decades, I had been comfortable with the family's traditional routine at home. After all, Germans like their routines. Organization, neatness, clarity, and precision were always the goal. The German mantra *Genauigkeit*, which is accuracy in all matters, wasn't looking good for this season. At a time when the fruits of my labor should be like vintage wine, the taste was more like vintage vinegar.

I loved the Dallas–Fort Worth area. We had a home in Arlington and a ranch in Glen Rose. I was settled in my Field Operations job that covered everything west of the Mississippi River, north to Alaska and all the way to Hawaii.

My much-loved neatness, clarity, and precision fell apart during the company's reorganization. In a two-week period, I considered two lucrative exit packages and had three internal company job offers. The drivers of this organization had obviously been imbibing a stronger beverage than coffee.

More than a little peeved, I sat in the human

resources corporate office in Denver and calmly suggested that our CEO had fifteen minutes to make up his mind. It took twenty-one minutes, but who was counting? The plan said I would work at Corporate and had to make my new home in Denver. This would not be good.

My daughter was in her junior year at the University of North Texas and lived in Denton. That was only thirty minutes from my old home, but it was a long way from Denver. My wife worked in Sales & Marketing with American Airlines / American Eagle. She travelled as much as I did, which was okay when we were together, but with me going through Denver and her going through DFW, we would do well to wave as we passed each other on the runways of various airports around the country. Fortunately, our Cairn Terrier, Scruffy, had departed earlier that year to the place where all good Cairn Terriers go—where I was sure he was driving the angels close to a nervous breakdown with his jovial antics.

I put together a plan. Remember, I'm all about precision. I put the house and ranch up for sale and rented a one-bedroom apartment in Denver. For three months, my wife and I practiced smiling and waving at each other as we passed. The Christmas season was coming, and I could see that maintaining family tradition was beyond the realm of possibility.

My wife phoned as I was getting off a flight in Phoenix. "I've decided to quit my job," she said. She was at American's operations facility in Chicago. "I've had enough. I want to turn in my resignation."

This was great news, although I had to do some quick mental gymnastics to determine how I would offset the loss of my D2 spousal airline pass. Our property in Texas still hadn't sold, but maybe it would soon. We decided we would put our furniture into storage and she would join me in my little Denver apartment in early December, just a few weeks away.

The Lord was working on his time schedule, not mine. Our house in Arlington sold and we closed in the next two weeks. Nice work, Sir! I wondered if he had missed the rest of my Christmas wish list. There was no prospect for selling the ranch.

I decided to fly our daughter up for Christmas. Since our living space in Denver was so limited, I reserved plush quarters in a condo at Copper Mountain, close to the main ski lift. That way, the family could spend Christmas as usual and have Santa turn into toast when he slid down our fireplace chimney. After some very close friends from Arlington reserved a condo only thirty feet away, I felt like my plan was really coming together

Besides having family and friends and escaping from corporate shenanigans, I looked forward to some serious snow skiing. I grew up in Zell im Wiesental, a small German town ten minutes by mountain railway from Feldberg in the Black Forest, where the elves reside—the little people known for their cuckoo clocks and ski slopes. I would strap on my hickories (all skis were made out of wood back then), ski two kilometers to the train station on my way to school in Schopfheim, and return late each day with the hickories strapped to my back next to my rucksack, filled with the books.

I looked forward to having my daughter at my side as we rooster-tailed fresh powder down the mountain. My wife, who had wrapped her skis around one of those Colorado pines years earlier, would pursue other demanding activities like shopping and keeping an appointment at the local spa.

We usually celebrated Christmas Eve in the old German tradition with a good dinner and an exchange of gifts, followed by a candlelight service at church. This year was different. My daughter and I slipped off the lift and onto the snow at 14,000 feet. We stopped long enough to have professional photographs taken and to be filled with awe at the wonders of God's creation. Ol' Dad tried to light his pipe, which I quickly learned was foolish at this altitude, in the cold, thin air. On the slopes we laughed and had fun like youngsters unwrapping presents on Christmas morning.

Already into a plan that was far from tradition, I made reservations for a dinner sleigh ride. The air was cold and crisp, our breath leaving a trail of fog, but we were bundled, snuggled close, and warm as we listened to the horse's hooves plop softly on the packed snow. As the air whistled through the trees, I could actually hear the snow when it fell from the limbs. How wonderful to hear the sound of peacefulness, void of cell phones and noise from machines and electrical devices. We were headed for an experience billed as "Dinner at a Miner's Tent," but I wasn't sure what to expect. I had visions of an old army tent with a steaming pot of beans over a campfire.

As we approached the tent, I wondered if any miner really lived like this. The tent was as big as a barn, with lanterns hanging down and two potbellied wood stoves throwing out heat. Rustic wood tables and benches for at least thirty people were set with fine china, linen napkins, more eating utensils than I knew how to use, and multiple wine glasses. Obviously, we were about to enjoy more than beef jerky and beans.

The atmosphere was much like a family reunion of traveling Gypsies. Our merry companions hailed from places all over the globe—England, the Netherlands, even South America—all coming for celebration on the eve of Christ's birth, with its promise of a better future. The musicians proved to be much more than their western attire suggested. They deftly played happy tunes like "Jingle Bells" and concluded with "Stille Nacht, Heilige Nacht."

On Christmas morning, I wasn't sure I wanted to return to the old tradition even if I could. We had made unforgettable memories together, and I had pictures to prove it. A simple life with simple joys provided wonderful relief from an avalanche of materialistic distractions and dissonant noises.

I decided home was wherever the heart finds comfort and trust in God's ability to bring peace in the midst of confusion.

No matter what tradition has been broken, every new year can be special.

Grandmom's Christmas Surprise
by Julie Cosgrove

After moving into our brand new duplex, I felt sure my husband and I would have our best Christmas ever. Our son, James, was almost three—the perfect age to enjoy the holidays and have wonderful, unforgettable memories. When the Big Freeze hit in 1982, I wasn't concerned.

Our duplex was so new I could still smell the freshness of the carpet and wallpaper we had picked out. Two huge bedrooms had walk-in closets. We had washer/dryer hook-ups and a fenced-in back yard. Unlike our neighbors, we even had a tree. A real fireplace was tucked diagonally in the corner of the living room, ideal for hanging Christmas stockings in anticipation of Santa's arrival. Conditions could not have been better.

Freezes do happen in Austin. Potted plants are brought in from the patio, the faucets are set to a slow drip, and bushes outside are draped with white sheets to resemble fat little ghosts. Usually by midmorning the next day, the eaves are dripping, the roofs no longer

33

have a fine sugar coating, and the grass doesn't crunch under foot.

Christmas Eve was our son's first year to participate in the church Nativity pageant. Because of his age, he got to be one of the sheep. Proud of our little wooly guy's performance, we drove home, all smiles.

At home, the frozen water pipes turned our smiles into worrisome concern. The meteorologists had forecast two more days before the temperature would climb above freezing. Until then, water wasn't available to drink, flush toilets, or take baths. I eyed the dirty dishes in the sink, the overflowing hamper in the hall, and my son's face, smudged with chocolate cupcake.

The phone rang. My husband grabbed it as I swallowed back the panic. How could we celebrate Christmas in our new home, much less survive any more long, frigid days like this one?

He mumbled sounds that didn't appear to answer anything and said, "You need to talk to Julie." He held out the receiver with that don't-talk-long look. "It's your mother. Her maternal antenna must have raised."

"Hi, Mom." I kept my tone even. "Listen, I really can't talk right now."

"What was Jerry saying?" Mom asked. "Did the pageant go okay? What's wrong?"

I told her.

"Can't y'all get down here to San Antonio? You can spend the night, and we can all wake up and have Christmas morning together after all."

Amid the hope in her voice, she sounded worried. No doubt, she missed having everyone together at the crack of dawn, excitedly tearing open presents. But this year, our son was in his first pageant. I wanted

34

Christmas morning around our own fireplace, with the logs crackling, our son giggling. It was time to leave old traditions and begin a new one.

I gave my husband a quizzical look. "I don't know, Mom. The roads may be iced over." From my expression and sounds on the phone, it didn't take a genius to know what my mother wanted. My husband knew. Her booming voice carried into the room.

Red-footed pajamas dangled under my husband's elbow as he vainly tried to stop our son's wiggling long enough to remove his fleece. "We can't leave now," he said. "The highways and bridges haven't been sanded. There's no telling when they will be."

James babbled questions in rapid succession, as youngsters do when full of sugary treats from post-pageant festivities. He ended his litany with "Hi Grandmom. Guess what I was tonight at church?"

"Hi. sweetie. I know. A sheep! I'm so proud of you." Her cheery voice was clear, even to my distant ear. When I took back the phone, she said, "You can't stay there, dear."

I paused to admire the twinkling tree and the stockings hanging from the fireplace mantle. "But Mom, it's our first Christmas here. We were all looking forward to… Oh, well. Here, talk with Jerry while I get James's jammies on."

I grabbed James and the footed pajamas. My husband took the phone.

While transforming the lamb back into a boy, I thought about the presents yet to be wrapped and the big one hidden in the closet. James would have been so excited to see it under our tree. Oh, how we'd scrimped and saved for it. Could we sneak it into the car and down to San Antonio without him knowing? Could we even get to San Antonio? If the roads were too hazardous, could we find a motel room? What if we became stranded at my parents' house? Who would feed the guinea pig and the cat? Should I pack more clothes? Did Mom have extra wrapping paper? Given time, I could have thought of a hundred reasons to stay home.

We decided the highways would be better now than later in the day. I busied James by letting him help pack, while my husband crammed presents into the trunk, covered with a quilt. We plopped the suitcases onto the back seat along with blankets, peanut butter sandwiches and bottled water, just in case.

James was used to sitting alone in the back. "Why is this stuff here?" he asked.

My husband winked at me. "It's freezing. I can't put them in the trunk."

"Oh, okay." James nodded, his curiosity satisfied.

With James in his car seat, we settled in for the long drive on icy roads, the vents blowing warm air. Just as we were about to creep onto the highway, a high-pitched voice bellowed, "But Santa won't know where I am!"

Anxious tears poured down his cheeks.

I unbuckled my seat belt, crawled over the suitcases, and hugged the blubbering child while my husband kept driving at a snail's pace. For countless slow, tedious miles, we talked about Jesus and how the wise men found *him*.

We prayed.

James sniffled.

We explained that Santa was a wise old soul who could find every good boy and girl.

My husband looked away from the road long enough to speak to James with confidence. "The stockings are in the suitcase, and we'll hang them up as soon as we get to Grandmom's."

Our red-faced son may not have been convinced, but he eventually fell asleep. Silent night. Holy night. All was calm, but not very bright.

After three hours of what should have been a forty-five minute trip, our car slipped and slid into the icy driveway at my parents' house, thanks to answered prayer and my husband's steeled resolve. The car's jerky movements woke our son.

When the headlights bounced off the garage door, he saw the sign and gasped. "Look, Mommy," he said. "A sign!"

Big bold letters were printed in my mother's handwriting. In laughter and tears, I read the words to James. "The sign says, *SANTA — JAMES IS HERE.* Isn't that wonderful?"

His eyes gleamed with delight. My husband squeezed my hand as an elderly woman wrapped in a quilt came with outstretched arms to greet us.

I love my mom.

Coffee and Pecan Pie
by Marty Norman

Sarah ignored the beauty of the enormous snow-flakes falling outside. All she saw was the ugliness of the bare floor where a Christmas tree should be. 'Still no money for presents," she said, mumbling to herself while searching for her keys. "Looks like Santa won't be coming this year."

No matter how she worked the math, the results came out the same. There wasn't any money to buy presents. How would she explain to the twins that Santa had passed them by? She didn't want to think about it, but she had no choice. Time was running out.

Sarah grabbed her ten-year-old coat and her purse. "Come on girls, or I'll be late for work. Let's get this show on the road."

The twins bounded down the stairs. Their happy voices brightened the darkness of her mood. How could she stay depressed when she was blessed with such delightful children?

The swish-swish of the wipers brushing the snow-flakes off the windshield added a beat to the girls' giggling and reminded her how fortunate she was to have them. After fifteen years of marriage, she and her husband, John, were ecstatic when she discovered she was expecting.

The pregnancy hadn't been easy. She fought nausea while being a secretary in the mornings and a waitress in the afternoons and evenings. Their insurance lapsed when John was laid off. If he hadn't found a part-time job with the post office, she didn't know what they would have done. They could barely make ends meet.

When the doctor put her to bed for the next three months, she tossed and turned with worry. How would they pay the bills? Worse yet, what if she lost the babies?

Amazingly, she carried the babies to term. They were perfect. They came home together, so filled with joy and anticipation, their lack of money didn't matter.

When she turned the corner toward the sitter's house, the snow came down heavier, making it hard to see the road and reminding her how difficult the last three years had been. With twice as many mouths to feed and diapers and baby clothes that were quickly outgrown, the bills kept piling up. Why was she complaining? No, it wasn't that. She wasn't complaining. The girls were wonderful, and they deserved a happy Christmas even if they couldn't have a tree.

The snowy roads made the drive to work take twice too long. She ran into the café, out of breath. "Sorry I'm late." She hung her coat on the wooden rack in the corner.

"Not to worry," Rudy said. "It's pretty slow with the snow and all."

She liked Rudy. He was flexible and easy to work for. Besides she could drop the girls at the sitter's on the way.

Business wasn't just slow. It was nearly non-existent. After each customer left, she counted her tips, hoping for enough to buy the two dolls at Blair's Department Store. Santa had promised the girls, and she couldn't bear the thought of breaking their hearts. By seven-thirty, she had collected only ten dollars—about half enough to pay for one doll. "Looks like Christmas will be even slimmer than I thought," she said to the tip money as she returned it to her pocket.

The wind blew the door open, and a snow-dusted customer came in, tall and thin with wavy brown hair. He pressed his weight against the door to close it after a flurry of snow and dried leaves blew in. Dressed only in a light windbreaker, he had to be a stranger to these parts, yet something about him seemed familiar. Maybe it was his manner, the way he brushed his hair from his eyes and carefully placed the windbreaker on the rack in the corner.

He plopped himself in the corner booth. "I'll take a cup of coffee and some pecan pie."

"Coming right up." While getting his order, she never took her eyes off him. There was something she couldn't put her finger on. He was about the age her brother, Tommy, would have been if he hadn't been killed by a sniper in Vietnam.

As she served the pie, she asked where he was headed. He was warm and friendly, and they struck up a conversation. He was on his way to visit his aunt in Sioux City, Idaho, but the snowstorm had made driving impossible.

"The motel has no vacancies," the stranger said. "I'll just wait out the storm here in the café if that's okay."

"The Café closes at ten o'clock," she said, "but I might have a better idea. Let me make a quick phone call." She returned after a few minutes. "I talked to my husband, John." She topped his coffee with a fresh brew. "He said he'd be mighty pleased if you'd stay in our guest room over the garage. It's a cold night and too treacherous to drive. My name's Sarah. We've used our garage a time or two as overflow, when the motel's full. John used to keep his tools there, but he had to pawn them. It's small but clean."

"That'd be great." He smiled. "I sure could use a warm bed. I've been driving twenty-six hours straight. And by the way, my name's Sam. I'm pleased to make your acquaintance."

"Hang around for a while." She headed back to mop the kitchen floor. "You can follow me home when my shift's over. I have just one stop on the way."

At ten o'clock, Sarah waved to Rudy and locked the door on her way out. Sam followed her to Blair's, a block away, and went inside. They were the only customers. Just for a moment, she wishfully fingered a wool coat on her way to the children's department. Forcing her eyes away from the doll department, she opted for a plastic table with two chairs for the girls. This would have to do. The price was right, marked down to ten dollars. Her tip money was just enough.

At the cash register, Sam looked impatient. "Could you give me your address? I need to get gas, so I can just meet you there."

"I'll leave the garage apartment unlocked," she

said. "It's been a long day, and I'm going to turn in. There's an extra blanket in the cupboard and a coffee maker on the bathroom shelf. Make yourself at home. If you need anything, come knock on the door."

No one knocked.

The next morning Sarah woke early. While tiptoe-ing down the stairs to make coffee, she saw the lighted Christmas tree and had to stop and catch her breath. Where did the tree come from? There it was, right where the bare floor had been the day before. Two dolls, just like the ones at Blair's, were sitting in the small plastic chairs she had bought. On the table between the dolls was a red wool coat and a set of tools. Had John received a bonus and played Santa dur-ing the night? Surely not. The post office didn't give bonuses.

A white envelope was hidden in the tree's branch-es. On the outside, in a man's handwriting, was the message: *Thanks for making a room at the inn. I tell you the truth, whatever you did for the least of these brothers, you did for me – Sam*

Inside were ten hundred-dollar bills. Wow! That was enough to pay bills for the next three months.

She looked out the window, but Sam's car was gone. To whom could she give thanks? The girls might think it was Santa, but the truth caused tears to stream down her face.

On the first Christmas morning, God sent the man Jesus to bless mankind. Two thousand years later, men were still doing his work.

"Glory to God in the highest" she said. "And on earth, peace, goodwill toward men."

Christmas Homecoming
by Jan Brand

Lindsey closed the door on the blowing snow outside and melted into the love seat in front of the fireplace. "Mother, the whole town is dressed up for Jeff's homecoming." Her excitement ended in a sigh.

"You sound tired." Mom got up from the couch and headed for the kitchen. "I'll make you some hot chocolate."

"No, I'm not tired. I'm too wound up to be tired. Dana and I got everything done at the church. We covered the chairs in cream-colored tulle and tied gold chrysanthemums on the backs with black velvet ribbon. The Christmas tree is a big Scotch pine hung with gold and black ornaments. It's Hardee High all over again, just like Jeff and I planned. Everything's done but meeting him at the train tomorrow."

"You still need something warm and cheery. It'll just take a moment."

Lindsey stared into the flickering flame, remembering. On a hot summer Texas afternoon, she had sidled up to the creek bank, trying to look nonchalant. Jeff

43

was the cutest boy she had ever seen. He told her, if she wanted to hang around with the guys, she had to put a wiggly worm on a hook. She would have *eaten* the worm to be with him. She took the disgusting thing and impaled it on a piece of metal shaped like a question mark. She was nine and he was eleven. From that day on, wherever he went, she wasn't far behind.

In junior high, he took her to the Sweetheart Dance. On the night of his senior prom, he gave her his class ring and they were officially going steady. In her mind they had been going steady from the moment she skewered the worm.

When only nine years old, she wanted to be Mrs. Jeff Baldwin. By the time she graduated from Hardee High, Jeff shared her dreams and asked her to marry him. He had just finished his sophomore year at A&M. Upon graduation he enlisted in the Marines, was commissioned a second lieutenant, and shipped out to the war in Afghanistan. He had that runaway American hero gene: love of God, country and family. She was proud of the man he had grown to be.

In a flurry of emails, they planned a wedding that would make a special memory for them and everyone in Hardee. His tour of duty was scheduled to end the week before Christmas. It was the perfect time to begin their lives together and celebrate with friends and relatives.

"Drink this. It'll warm you up." Mom set a steaming mug on the lamp table and bustled off to do laundry.

The front door opened. "Yoo-hoo." Dana waltzed in, arms waving, twirling around with a big smile on her face. "Have you ever seen Hardee look so beautiful?

Every tree and lamp post is tied with gold ribbon. The town looks like one big Welcome Home present."

Lindsey grinned. Everything sounded wonderful, but she hadn't expected anything less from the good folk of Hardee. Several friends had helped her decorate the tree at church, and instead of having a catered affair, the ladies insisted they provide the food. Who could resist these Texas cooks turning out their prized recipes for Jeff's homecoming?

The big day dawned bitter cold and sunny. Lindsey held her wedding dress in front of her and looked into the mirror. A tear slid down her face. The white silk shantung gown glimmered with seed pearls and irides- cent beads that covered the tight-fitting bodice in a pat- tern of dainty flowers. It was like a fairy princess dress. When Mom took her all the way to Dallas to buy it, all she could think about was how Jeff would stand in his Marine uniform and look at her when she walked down the aisle.

Mom opened the door and stuck her head in. "Honey, can I help you with your dress?"

"Yes, thanks. I don't want to get blush or mascara on it."

Mom placed the wide skirt on the floor so Lindsey could step into it. She pulled up the dress and zipped the back.

Lindsey gave a pleasure-filled sigh, glad she had resisted Mom's advice to not put on the dress until she got to church. Wearing it to the train station was the perfect choice. "I hope the train's on time so everyone doesn't freeze."

"Oh, honey, I don't think anyone will mind."

Her father's voice came through the closed door.

"Lindsey, it's time to go."

Jeff's Marine buddies would be at the train station to form an honor guard. At the church, they would line the walkway with their swords aloft. It was the highest honor they could pay one of their own.

The living room was filled with people who wanted to caravan to the train station. When their white limousine reached Main Street, her mascara began to run. Every few feet, a Hardee flag-waver stood ready to welcome their hero back. Near the courthouse, veterans stood with the Boy Scouts, poised for a salute when the caravan returned. Then there were all the young men and women with whom she and Jeff had grown up, some holding bundled babies in their arms, others with toddlers at their side. Parents and grandparents were there—all the good folk of Hardee—each holding a tiny American flag. The limo moved slowly, allowing her to wave to everyone.

At the train station, the high school band was already playing "God Bless America." The limo passed the police motorcycles that would be their escort. Lindsey got out and walked with Mom, Dad, and Dana to the platform.

A distant train whistle sounded.

Jeff would soon be home. She hugged Jeff's parents, feeling like she had always been part of their family.

Jeff's mom wore a peach wool dress. Jeff always told her how pretty she looked in peach. He was right. Her auburn hair looked so much like his, and with her chocolate brown eyes, peach was definitely her color.

The distant clatter became a deafening roar before the train came to a stop. The whistle sounded one last time. Marines filed out of a passenger car. The crowd waited patiently while the honor guard took their place. Then the band struck up the Marine hymn and everyone stood at attention.

The trainmen opened the big metal door. Six Marines took hold of the flag-draped coffin, lifted it onto their shoulders, walked across the platform and down the steps, and loaded it onto the caisson.

Lindsey took her place beside the casket in the procession toward the church. Family and friends followed. The band played "I'll Be Home for Christmas" as they walked in-cadence down Main Street. Everything was as she hoped it would be. Jeff would be proud.

Jeff Baldwin had come home to the people who loved him. Today would soon be gone, but the memories would last forever. With the townspeople's help, she would look to the future and new relationships, but Jeff would forever be her first love.

Colliding Moons
by Jon Jacobs

Both moons hung low in the afternoon sky as McCauley Flynn sprinted across the campus. Mac glanced at Copra, the distant, orange moon, already taken by the Androsians. If these gargantuan bird-like creatures captured Silbra, their large silvery moon, a thousand years of pleasure-seeking and technological advancement on Tetrazan would be lost. It was time for war.

Mac raced up the steps, taking two at a time. The Christmas flora and its sweet smell reminded him of their tradition, passed down from the ancients who lived on Earth. Today they needed a real savior, one who could lead the fight with something more forceful than psychology. Otherwise, their world, admittedly chaotic because of its self-serving nature and moral degradation, would be a fading memory. He wondered if the Biblia contained any battle plans. He should ask his priester about that.

Just three parlics before start time, Mac walked into his class and touched the big screen to begin his lecture. At the top, the heading: *Welcome to Propulsion Engineering 101.* The control monitor registered the names of all fifteen draftees, present and on time, plus two men and one woman online, attending the class remotely.

"I'm Lieutenant Flynn, your instructor today." Any hairy, long-armed beast could have made the presentation if the programming techs could find a way to connect meaningful responses to a draftee's unpredictable questions. "You all know why you're here, so let's get started."

One student raised his hand.

"Yes, uh…" Mac glanced at monitor to find the name of the youngster sitting at seat 3D. "Mr. Nieland, if you want to ask me something, press the yellow button, the one with the question mark."

No response.

"Mr. Nieland, I'm waiting. Are you going to press the button?" Mac was not about to explain the necessity of pressing the button so their dialogue would be recorded and evaluated.

"Oh, sorry." Nieland pressed the button. "Why *are* we here?"

"It was in your orientation. Every newscast has predicted this war. You better learn to pay attention. Wake up, all of you, or you'll bring destruction to your cruiser, if not the whole world." He tapped a button. A new slide appeared on the screen. "This is the fusion reactor, affectionately known as the Star Power Unit because it fires a propulsion beam the same way stars generate power. Each unit sends a three-gigawatt blast. You have four of these units mounted on your craft."

Mac paused briefly, long enough to allow a

pressing question but not enough parlics for a mindless student to organize his ignorance and ask something stupid. They just needed to listen.

Next slide.

A knock, and the door cracked open. Colonel Jason Umbry, motioning him to come.

"A moment please." Mac pointed at the screen. "Simulator training begins in eight partas. By then you must know all twenty-seven procedures, backward and forward." He stepped out of the room.

Before Mac could protest the inconvenience that could have been avoided with a simple call on his monitor, Colonel Umbry held up his hand. "I needed you out of the room. Your reaction might have been read by the students."

"What reaction?"

"You're to be on Sibra one parta before the crossing of the moons." The colonel pointed toward the classroom. "With your crew."

"That's not enough time. We've barely started—"

"You don't understand. We're *out* of time. The Androsians aren't waiting until we're ready to send them an invitation."

Twenty-nine partas later, Mac was strapped in his seat, praying for a miracle. How could he command a draftee crew who, with one miscalculated press of a button, would take them into eternity? Instead of their Christmas tradition, his family would grieve his death. He counted down the time as he watched the moons, now closer in their orbits. The final parlics: *ten, nine, eight…* He closed his eyes when the thrust pressed him deep into his seat and stretched the skin tight on his face.

50

Mac took a deep breath. The brilliance of the stars, the clouds and deep blue seas when he looked toward Tetrazan, the freedom he felt in weightlessness—no matter how many times he spaced, the breathtaking feeling was always there as he considered God's wisdom and power. Most people on Tetrazan questioned God's existence. Not Mac. Space travelers got to experience the divine point of view.

The sun's reflection on Silbra's mountain snow created shining rings around its silver craters. The bright, almost-white, moon filled half the viewing screen. Dark, dry, and barren Copra, up and to the right, would soon be eclipsed, called *Kolidmonden*—the colliding of the moons. This event happening at Christmas used to be important, but as war replaced hope for peace, *Kolimonden* had lost its significance.

Mac glanced at the navigator, then the engineer. "All set for entry." No! The descent was all wrong. A three-gigawatt blast from Reactor Number Four had taken them off-course, away from Silbra, toward Copra. "You hit the wrong button," Mac yelled. "Compensate."

"I can't." The navigator pressed the triangular button twice. "The controls aren't responding."

"What is our heading?"

"Nothing, sir. We're not moving at all."

The viewing screen went blank. With the cruiser floating in space, Mac felt entombed.

Light filled the cabin, drawing everyone's attention to the screen. The Androsians. The forward creature's white wings filled the screen, spread wide but not moving, yet he appeared to be suspended in the air. An army of winged creatures rose behind him, as far as the

51

eye could see—thousands of them.

"You are in violation of your own code." The leader's voice echoed, his tone amplified by the entire host.

Mac hoped the recorder was running, because Androsians had been seen but no one had ever heard them speak.

"Your ancients gave you the message. Why have you not listened? Have you not seen the consequence of going your own way?" The leader paused as the smooth melodies of many voices rose and then faded. "Behold, I remind you of the good news that should have brought joy to all your people. The anointed child came not to receive but to give, to bring peace and goodwill to all men. Go. Tell your stories. Turn the hearts of the people from helping themselves to doing what they can to help others. In this you will find peace in the midst of turmoil."

The screen went black. Then their view of space returned. Copra's terrain showed no signs of life.

"What did he say?" the engineer asked. "What stories are we to tell?"

"I don't know," Mac said. "Without pictures, no one would believe this has happened." He pressed the button to replay the video. Nothing. No picture. No voice. With the volume turned all the way up, he could hear singing, but the words were foreign, unlike anything on Tetrazan.

"It appears, in all these years, we've lost sight of the meaning of Christmas," Mac said. "Maybe our stories are needed for people to believe."

Two Tickets
by Christine Thomas

For most people, a gift of two tickets to a Dallas Cowboys football game would be wonderful. Not for me, not when the game was on Christmas day. I wanted to be with my family, but I couldn't be with everybody. What was I going to do?

Dad sounded excited when he said, "Your mom and I want to do something different this year." He wanted his kids and their spouses to join him for a great family time at the game.

I was stuck between two good choices: I could go to a game or spend the holiday with my husband's parents as we had already planned. I rapidly twirled the pros and cons in my mind like a Rubik's Cube, wishing the solution would magically appear.

"We'll all have a great time," Dad said, obviously excited. "You'll get to see the new stadium. To get the six of us seated together, I need to buy the tickets now."

"Wow, Dad. That's really generous." I tried to share his enthusiasm. "Paul will probably want to go, but since we already made plans, let me talk to him and get back with you."

I hung up the phone, feeling like a shaken can of soda. Would Dad's idea add bubbly fizz to our holidays or explode in a sticky mess?

"We should go to the game," my husband said. "My parents will understand." He thought watching the Cowboys play under the dome of the "eighth wonder of the world" was a gift to remember.

"Okay, I'll call Dad." I picked up the phone, then set it back down. "Uh... what about the kids?" They were too young to leave at home alone. My in-laws lived too far away to take them for the day, and nobody would be willing to babysit, not on Christmas Day. My dad hadn't offered to pay for any grandkids, and I knew we couldn't afford the $400 for the extra seats. "You can go without me," I said. "I'll stay with the kids."

I wanted to make memories with my brother and my parents, but the kids were more important to me than a football game. I described how wonderful it would be to prepare a holiday meal while he went to see the Cowboys play.

A hint of disappointment on my husband's face quickly became a look of resolve. "This is your parents' gift to both of us. As much as it pains me to turn down their generous, awesome, unforgettable, life-changing offer—"

I cleared my throat, prompting him to make his point.

"I'm not going without you, and I will not spend Christmas Day without my children."

He really wanted to go. I knew he did, so I repeated my arguments, louder this time, with more animation. "One of us has to go. How would Dad feel if we both turned him down?"

"In that case," Paul said, "you should be the one to go. I'll stay home. It's your family and a once-in-a-lifetime chance to make a lasting memory with your father."

Was he just saying that, or did he really want me to go? I couldn't tell. I faced a call to duty, but which was higher, "Honor thy mother and father," or "Wives, submit to your husbands?"

On my wedding day, I made a commitment to my husband, but I wasn't sure what he wanted. Since my dad had been diagnosed with cancer, any time I could spend with him was important. Some of my dad's bold choices showed his intention to live his life to its fullest. While buying Cowboys tickets on Christmas Day wasn't as dramatic as his cherry-red T-top Corvette, I suspected he was trying to create an unforgettable holiday experience with his grown children. How could I deny him that, yet still honor my husband's desire to keep our own family together?

We sparred a while longer, but the match ended in a draw. Meanwhile my Dad texted to say my brother and sister-in-law were on board. Oh great. Now I was the one who would ruin the party if I didn't go.

Saying yes to one part of my family meant saying no to another, so somebody would be unhappy, no matter which choice I made. Unable to decide, I asked what the Lord wanted me to do. The kids wouldn't carry emotional scars for life if we spent one Christmas apart. And if I wasn't sitting at the stadium with my dad, he wouldn't plunge into depression. I wouldn't miss God with either choice, so what should I do?

I picked up the phone and dialed the home where I'd spent half my life's Christmases.

"So what'd you decide?" he immediately asked.

"Well, Dad I don't mean to disappoint you. We really appreciate your offer, but here's the thing..." I launched into my internal struggle and the ultimate duty I felt to keep *my* family together on Christmas Day. I needed to honor the plans we had already made with my in-laws.

"It's okay, Christine. I understand." He spoke with an unmistakable tone of disappointment.

I wilted, wavering in my decision. "Well, I... um... I guess..."

"Hey, it's okay. What do you say we come to town a few days early and celebrate Christmas with you, Paul, and the kids then?"

I swallowed the lump in my throat. "Yeah, Dad. That sounds like a great idea."

On Christmas Day, I'd be thinking about my parents and my brother, huddled in that enormous stadium, eating greasy concession food and laughing about the out-of-control fans two rows down. But if I had chosen to be with my dad, then I'd be thinking about what I was missing at my in-laws' house, unable to watch the eager faces of my children as they ripped colorful wrapping from a gift they just had to have.

My dad was right. It was okay.

We couldn't all be together at the same time, but we were together at different times. I learned that we could celebrate on any day at any place, because the holidays needed only the opportunity to connect with those we love. When the time and locations aren't that important, we don't have to buy tickets.

When Herald Angels Sing
by Joan Hall

Ten-year-old Brigitte Dawson stepped off the school bus into a cold north wind, eager for more than Mama's steaming homemade cookies. She wanted Mama to be well again so she could come to her performance in the Christmas play at church.

She pulled the hood of her jacket over her curly blond hair, thinking how wonderful it would be to look down from the choir and see Mama's smiling face looking up at her. How long had it been since she saw Mama really smile—the kind of smile that lit up the room?

Forever.

She quickened her pace down the long driveway to the house, believing for fresh chocolate-chip cookies. With Thanksgiving only a week away and Christmas a month later, little time was left for believing Mama would get better.

On Thanksgiving weekend two years ago, Brigitte's older brother, Mark, had died in a car crash. After the funeral, Mama locked herself in Mark's room, refused

57

to come out, and wouldn't let anybody in. Later, when Pastor Briggs came to visit, she ignored all the rules of hospitality. "Don't come back," she said. Her tone was harsh, filled with anger. "I don't want anything to do with church. If God loved me, he wouldn't have taken my only son."

Would this Christmas be as bad as that one?

No one had felt like celebrating. They didn't decorate a Christmas tree or exchange gifts. Daddy took Brigitte and her sister Trish to Aunt Vivian's house because Mama didn't want anything to do with a Christmas dinner with family. She stayed home, refusing to see anyone. The next day, Daddy took her to a doctor.

When spring arrived, the coldness in Mama's heart seemed to warm with the melting snow. For the first time in months, she smiled a little. Aunt Vivian helped her clean out Mark's things so they could be donated to the orphanage. She appeared to be much better, that is, until Daddy asked her to go with him to church.

"No! Not if Hell freezes over." Her bitterness showed in her fiery eyes. "I'm not going to any church. You can take Brigitte and Trish."

By autumn, Mama was as deep in depression as before. No, deeper. Many days, Brigitte came home from school and found Mama crying uncontrollably.

One night, men in white uniforms came in an ambulance and took Mama to the hospital. She stayed away for a long time.

A year passed. Mama had her good days and bad days. Mostly bad.

Today didn't appear to be any better. Brigitte prayed, but her prayers weren't working.

A few days after Thanksgiving, she walked into the house and found Aunt Vivian sitting at the kitchen table with Daddy. Aunt Vivian looked up and wiped the tears from her eyes. Daddy straightened his drooping shoulders.

"Where's Mama?" Brigitte asked. "Is she okay?"

"Aunt Vivian will take you to church this evening," Daddy said.

"Did Mama go away again?"

"Yes, honey. She went to the hospital."

"I don't want anything to happen to Mama." Brigitte took her turn, crying. "I want her to get better."

Aunt Vivian wrapped her arms around Brigitte. "We all want that, sweetheart. In the meantime, you can stay with Uncle James and me."

"But I want Mama to come to my Christmas play." Brigitte broke into tears again. Clearly, there was no hope if she was in the hospital. "If she gets to come home, will she be well enough to see me in the choir? She won't go to church. But she would come to see me sing, wouldn't she?"

"Honey," Daddy said in a consoling tone, "we'll have to wait and see."

Two weeks before Christmas, Mama came home. She seemed to be doing a little better.

Aunt Vivian stayed with Mama during the day and helped Trish decorate the Christmas tree. "You kids will have a real Christmas this year," she said.

Most of the time, Mama kept to herself, but Daddy convinced her to come to the table for dinner. She didn't talk to anyone. After eating only a few bites, she went back to her room.

With Christmas almost here, Brigitte didn't want to

59

ask, fearing what Mama would say, but she couldn't wait any longer. "Mama"—she waited for recognition, but got none—"will you please come to my Christmas play at church?"

No smile.

Brigitte could have waited one more day. She wished she had. "Mama, please. I'm singing in the choir. We have shepherds and wise men, Mary and Joseph, and of course, the baby Jesus."

"How dare you ask that of me?" Her expression was like somebody had slapped her. "No, I won't watch some fairytale play. God isn't real," she shouted. "If he existed, he wouldn't have taken my son. Leave me alone. I want to see my son, nobody else." Mama began to sob.

In tears, Brigitte ran to her room upstairs. Trish and Daddy must have heard the commotion, because they were in her room soon afterward.

Daddy wrapped his arms around Brigitte and Trish, and they wept together.

"I don't know what to do for your mother anymore," Daddy said. "The accident did more than take Mark's life. It took a little of your mother as well. I love you girls. I want you both to know that. Mama loves you too. She'll come around some day. We'll all get through this."

Brigitte couldn't sleep. She tried to pray, but couldn't. Someday Mama might get better, but not this Christmas.

Voices came from downstairs, but not loud enough to hear what was said.

She crept into the hallway to listen. Arguing. Daddy saying something about the way Mama treated everyone. Mama crying. Daddy sounded frustrated, saying he didn't know what else to do.

Mama's heart was as cold as the winter night.

Brigitte sat at the top of the stairs, bowed her head, and whispered, "Please God. Make Mama better. She doesn't think you're real, but I know Mark is in Heaven with you. He wouldn't want Mama to be so sad. It's okay if Mama doesn't come to my play. I just want her to get well."

When the night of the play arrived, Aunt Vivian came early to take Brigitte to church so Daddy could bring Trish later.

When the lights dimmed, Brigitte walked onto the stage with the choir. Where was Daddy? The organ played, and the choir began the heavenly chorus: *Hark the Herald Angels Sing.* There he was, in the fourth row, two seats from Trish, but who was between them? Her jaw dropped. Mama?

Yes! It was Mama. Her smile broke through the darkness, warming Brigitte's heart.

After the play, Mama welcomed Brigitte with open arms. "I love you so much, honey."

"I love you too, Mama. I prayed for you to get better, but I never dreamed you would come. God answered my prayer."

"You prayed for me?"

"Yes Mama, I did."

Another smile. This time, even brighter. "Oh, honey, I'm so sorry. How can people forgive me for being so selfish?" She glanced toward Pastor Briggs, standing nearby. "Will God forgive me?"

"Yes, he does." Brigitte spoke before Pastor Briggs could answer. "See that baby in the manger? He came

61

to forgive us."

"How can you be so sure?"

"Don't you know? He died on the cross for our sins. All this time he has felt your pain."

"Really?"

"Yes, Mama. God understands how it feels to lose a son."

Dustbowl Days
by Rhodema A. Cargill

Teaching kids in a one-room rural schoolhouse was only temporary until Betty Hollowell could find her beau, get married, and have a family. It wouldn't be easy because that was the goal of most single ladies in the 1930s, and these were hard times, living in the Oklahoma dustbowl.

She thought the drought couldn't get worse until the area went three months without a drop of rain. Crops were failing. Cattle were dying. Most of the parents were worried whether they would keep their farms.

One spring morning, after Betty dismissed her students for lunch and to play outside, Wanda Johnson stopped at her desk. "Teacher," she said, "I'm sorry I was late. I didn't mean to cause a fuss." She was one of her favorite students. Wanda walked barefoot to school each morning with her three younger brothers.

"I'm sure you had a good reason."

"Yes, teacher, Mama birthed a baby early this morning. I got a sister this time." Wanda's eyes shone with delight.

"Is your mother well? What about the baby?"

"Emma Marie is beautiful. Mama says she's pretty as me." Wanda giggled. "Mama is tired, but a neighbor woman came to sit with her when Papa went to work. I got the boys here. I'm sorry we was late."

Wanda grabbed her lunch pail and skipped outside.

Betty sighed and stepped to the window. The thin figure crossed the schoolyard as the wind whipped her dress around her ankles and tugged at the bow in her hair. She joined her three brothers, who sat under the lone shade tree in the whirling dust. Babies should be a blessing, but another mouth to feed wasn't always good news these days.

After all the children left, Betty locked the schoolroom door and drove to Fielder's Drugstore where she picked out a pink blanket and a baby comb-and-brush set. The clerk gift-wrapped the box with pink paper, a ribbon, and a bow.

The Johnson's farmyard was mostly dry dirt and dust. A few weeds grew around the edges of the sagging porch and alongside the outhouse. The clapboard house sorely needed a fresh coat of paint. The creak when Betty's foot hit the first step brought Wanda to the door.

"Teacher's here," Wanda shouted, swinging the screen door open wide. She led Betty to the back room.

Mrs. Johnson lay in bed with a tiny bundle next to her. She ran a pale hand through her thin hair that had begun to gray far too early.

Betty handed her the gift.

Thank you," Mrs. Johnson said, accepting the package. "Would you like to hold Emma?"

Betty was used to holding dolls, not babies. She

cradled Emma in her arms, dreaming of what it would be like to hold a real, live doll of her own. Emma's miniature rosebud lips formed into a yawn. She stared into Betty's eyes without blinking, and Betty couldn't look away. Betty's heartbeat doubled when Emma's tiny hand gripped her little finger.

Soon afterward, Betty's beau, Carl, proposed. It wasn't proper for married ladies to work, so they planned the wedding for the day after school was out.

During the last day of school, tears often filled Betty's eyes. These were her kids, and she would never see them again. She wondered who they would become. She probably would never know. She hugged each student and said goodbye. Wanda squeezed her hard and didn't want to let go. For the last time, she locked the classroom door, ready to have a family of her own.

Carl and Betty moved to the next county, where he kept the farm and taught at the government school for Indian children. She busied herself keeping their home, praying for a child of their own.

For three years, the house remained empty. That pain turned to joy when she found out she was pregnant. The pain returned with a vengeance when she lost the baby and the doctor said she would never be able to bear children. Deep depression set in. She wasn't sure she wanted to live. A hundred times she prayed, asking God why. A hundred times she received no answer.

Finally, she vowed to be content. And most of the time she was, but some days, the longing for a child was overwhelming and the tears flowed.

As the first Christmas approached after their loss, gray clouds hung over the cold, barren fields around the farmhouse, perfectly matching her mood. Too sad to concentrate on housework, she decided to drive into town. She parked on Main Street, in front of the grocery store. At the toy store next door, three children had their faces pressed against the glass, apparently anticipating what they might get for Christmas. With her head down, Betty hurried to buy groceries. Otherwise, she would have cried.

In small country towns, people knew one another and just about everything about everyone in the area. News traveled fast—especially about people's misfortunes. While looking for a good head of lettuce, Betty overheard a lady say something about the Johnson tragedy.

"What? Please tell me," she said. "I taught Wanda and her three younger brothers."

"Up and left, that's what that no-account man done," the lady said.

"He went out one morning and hightailed it out of there," the other lady said. "Never did come home. Left all of those mouths to feed on that dry, dusty farm."

The lady near Betty said, "Mrs. Johnson had to parcel out her children to strangers and go to work."

"What about Emma?" Betty asked. "She would be almost five now."

No one knew.

Betty drove to the school office to see the superintendent, still there from her teaching days. He would know.

"She's in a foster home," he said.

"Can she—can she be adopted?" She blurted the question without thinking, but as soon as the words erupted from her mouth, she knew that's what she wanted to do. Was it possible?

66

"I don't know." He wrote down the name of the foster home. "I believe this is where she is. I can't tell you the circumstances."

Carl was as good at moving the legal system as he was hard-working. Within weeks, they received the exiting news. The judge scheduled Emma's arrival a few days before Christmas.

Betty kept running to the front window, watching for the car to arrive. Just before dusk, the social worker drove up. She carried a small suitcase and held Emma's hand as they walked up the steps.

Emma's dark curls bounced, and her eyes sparkled when she saw the Christmas tree in the corner of the living room. Of course, she had no way of knowing most of the packages under the tree had her name on them.

After tucking Emma into bed, Betty opened Emma's suitcase to put up her belongings. At the bottom was the pink blanket and comb-and-brush set Betty had given to her when she was a baby.

Through her tears, Betty looked up and thanked God for his wonderful gifts. On this Christmas, all the poverty and pain of the dustbowl days turned to joys of abundant refreshing and rain.

Christmas Chill
by Cynde Hauser

The busy Christmas season kept me moving non-stop all day. Late that evening after work, I barely had enough energy to pick up my baby, Summer, from the sitter and see her safely snuggled in her bed. After pouring a glass of apple juice, I turned on the television in the living room, thinking I could unwind. It wasn't enough.

I walked into my bedroom and plopped on top of the covers, kicking off my shoes, with no thought for changing clothes. Not yet. My pillow welcomed me with the rest I craved, so I closed my tired, burning eyes to relax for a minute.

The television was still on in the living room, showing a Christian program I often watched from start to finish. Not tonight. I just listened to the man's calm reassurance: "God loves you and…"

Groggily, I came to my senses enough to know I had been asleep. What had awakened me? My thoughts went to Summer, who must be close to wanting her bottle. She wasn't crying though. She wasn't making a sound.

Still half asleep, I rolled over and closed my eyes again, seeing a strange man standing over me, watching me from the end of my bed, mostly hidden in the darkness but clearly visible in my dream. Who was he?

Thunk!

The noise awakened me with a start, and I listened to hear it again. Nothing. Immediately I knew Summer was up, expecting me to get her bottle. I stumbled out of bed and shuffled into the kitchen. The kitchen floor felt like ice to my bare feet. Why was the room so cold? As I reached into the refrigerator, I felt a chilly breeze, not from inside, but from the living room. Was I still dreaming? No, this was real, but why was it so cold? The heater must have quit working.

I walked into the living room where my full glass of apple juice was still resting on the coffee table. Summer's blanket was draped over the rocking chair. The window was open. Why? It should be closed and locked.

I froze with a shocking realization. Someone had come through the window into my apartment. I wasn't dreaming. A man really had been standing at the foot of my bed, looking down at me.

I looked past the television. At another time, the televangelist's ramblings might have interested me, but not now. In the corner of the room, the Christmas tree lights were flashing red, green, and yellow. I'd left everything on when I went to my bedroom, thinking I would turn them off when I got ready for bed.

When my gaze went to the bottom of the tree, I gasped. The presents were gone—all of them. Only the bare floor surrounded the tree. "Oh, my God!"

I set Summer's bottle on the coffee table and backed toward the only door in and out of my apartment, looking around as I moved. How could a man have come through my upstairs window? Did he leave the same way or was he still here? He could be in Summer's room, watching her like he had watched me. I listened for any sound from her room. Nothing. If I entered her room and he was there, we could both be dead.

I looked at the phone, thinking I should call 9-1-1, but the man might hear me. I needed to get help from outside. I eased the door open, ran to my neighbor's apartment, and pounded on his door.

Dave looked as if he sensed my panic. "Cynde, what's wrong?"

"Someone broke into my apartment. He was standing over me. All the presents are gone. I need to make sure Summer's okay."

Like a soldier ready for hand-to-hand combat, Dave grabbed his baseball bat. "Come on. Let's go."

Summer's crying brought me immediate comfort. She was cold and upset that no one had come to her aid. With tears in my eyes, I reached for her, held her tightly in my arms, and thanked God she was safe.

After Dave checked every room, he closed the window and offered to feed Summer while I called the police.

The investigating officer asked an endless string of questions while his associates looked for clues. They dusted for fingerprints and looked for anything the burglar might have left behind. They opened every closet and examined the floors.

"Ms. Bingham," the officer said, "You're sure

lucky. When that man stood over your bed, staring at you, he was deciding what to do with you. Most burglars would run as soon as they saw somebody at home. They might grab a few things on the way out, but they wouldn't stop and look you over."

I understood his message. I was lucky to be alive. The thought of what might have happened to me and my baby made my hands tremble.

"If you hadn't fallen asleep in your clothes," he said, "or the Christian program hadn't been on your television, this could have been more than a burglary. If you had awakened and screamed—if you had challenged him—if you had even acknowledged his presence, he could have dealt you serious harm. This scene could have been a rape or a homicide. Seems like someone was looking out for you tonight." He gave me a copy of his report and motioned for his men to follow him out the door.

I sat on the couch, cuddling Summer, thinking how blessed we were. The lights on the Christmas tree were still flashing on and off. The gifts were gone, but that didn't matter because I still held my most precious treasure in my arms.

The window was closed. The apartment was warming up, but that wasn't what took away the Christmas chill. Like the baby Jesus who was safe in the manger, Summer and I were safe because our lives were in God's hands.

To Ana With Love
by Lisa Bell

With a glance at the clock, Leo wished it was closing time so he could finish Ana's gift, his last hope for
improving his relationship with his daughter. The busy
holidays were great for his jewelry business. It also
helped get his mind off his wife's death earlier in the
year, but he had little time to make gifts.

Leo shortened his conversation with his customer.
"Thank you, Bill." He placed the velvet box in friend's
hand. "I'm sure your sweet wife will love her ring."

No more customers. No more friends.

He went to the front door, locked it, and turned
the sign to *Closed*. He hadn't planned to close early, but
this was Christmas Eve and he was out of time.

At his work bench, he unwrapped the polished
stone, found by accident. Ana would love it because it
came from where they went camping when she was
little. At first glance, it looked like any shiny rock, but as
light fell onto the surface, a rainbow beamed onto the
workroom wall.

He selected the finest gold setting—simple, yet

elegant, with natural ocean-jasper beads gracing a dainty chain. He reached for a closure.

No. That won't do. Such a fine piece must have a special clasp.

He rummaged through the drawer and held up a heart shaped fastener. *Perfect. A heart for the love of my heart.* The extraordinary stone, mounted on a swirled connector, created the focal point of the necklace. The beads between two-inch lengths of chain complemented the stone without distraction.

His hands ached and his eyes burned from working with so many tiny pieces, but he was almost finished. While he secured the finishing rings and heart clasp, church bells announced the midnight services. He dropped the pendant into its velvet box and closed the lid.

Ana will treasure this. She has to. I need her now. We need each other.

With the velvet box in his pocket, he switched off the light and stepped into the night, entering the church with bright expectations for the morning. Indeed, this would be a merry Christmas.

Ana woke early, expecting the smell of turkey in the oven. Mom always cooked the turkey overnight, and the smell woke her long before sunrise. This time, she was shaken by the missing smell, a reminder that Mom wasn't there.

Oh, Mom, I miss you so much. I worry about Dad. He stays late at the shop and barely eats. I wish you were here. I don't even know how to cook a turkey.

While wiping the tears from her eyes, she started the coffee maker.

A knock at the back door.

Who could that be? Not Dad. Yes, probably, but this early? Just show up. Don't think to call. That was Dad, off in his own world, never considering her feelings.

She opened the door to see her father, arms loaded with presents. "Dad, what are you doing, spending so much money?"

"I didn't spend much. I've been busy creating gifts with my own hands." His eyes twinkled. "Well, don't just stand there. Help me get them under the tree before my grandchildren wake up."

"How did you find time?" She tried not to sound suspicious. "Every time I called the shop, you were too busy to talk."

As they placed the last package under the tree, Tina and Terry bounced into the room, full of hugs and giggles, as if their grandmother hadn't been missed.

Ana thought, *This isn't right*, but didn't say anything.

Wrapping paper flew around the room, in less than half an hour reducing months of shopping to a stash of clothes and toys. The kids' joyful shrieks reminded her of days when she was little, hugging Mom, laughing and saying thank you. Tears stung her eyes as she swallowed hard and went to the kitchen for more coffee.

Dad followed. "Princess, one more gift. I made this for you." His face glowing, he handed her a velvet box.

Who was he calling princess? He hadn't called her that since she was little. She peeked inside the box. "Oh, nice. A shiny rock."

"Not just any rock. Remember that place where we loved to camp when you were a girl?"

Ana nodded, seeing gigantic trees, cool forests, and long hikes. She choked at the thought of Mom bringing marshmallows, chocolates, and graham crackers to make smores. "You would hold the marshmallow just above the fire until that golden brown crust produced the perfect flavor."

"I went back there last week. This stone was right in my path—waiting for me to pick it up. The beauty was hidden inside, just needing to be polished and brought into the light. God made this especially for you."

"Dad, you shouldn't have gone out there alone. You could have hurt yourself." She held the necklace away from her, not sure she wanted it. "Besides, all this gold and fancy gems. It's too expensive."

"You're my only daughter," Dad said, sounding disappointed, tears filling his eyes. "I wanted to make a special gift for you."

"It's nice, Dad. Really." She feared crying if she said anymore, thinking, *why can't Mom be here?*

"I'm sorry you don't like it."

"It's not that. It's beautiful." She turned the stone in her hand. "You know I don't wear jewelry. It's such an extravagant gift."

"Love should be extravagant," he whispered. "God gave the most extravagant gift of all on that first Christmas. He brought salvation to the world."

"I know." She sighed and wrapped her arms around him, trying to make up for hurting him.

The remainder of the day passed with a semblance of joy, but the wounded look in his eyes haunted her

75

long after he had left. He did love her, perhaps too much.

Late that night, the phone rang.

"Ana, this is Bill." His tone was soft, hardly more than a whisper. "I went to see Leo, to tell him how happy Sue was with…" His voice trailed into sobs. "Ana… sweetheart… your dad has suffered a massive heart attack. The medics are with him, but he's gone. I'm so sorry."

Ana collapsed on the floor, surrounded by his gifts. The velvet box was on the coffee table, right there where she had left it. Hands trembling, she removed the pendant and studied the intricate detail. She pictured her dad bent over his workbench. He must have worked for many hours to create the perfect gift. As she turned the stone, the Christmas lights cast a rainbow of colors across the room. She pulled the pendant to her heart, treasuring extravagant love.

What had Dad said? *God made this especially for you.* She squeezed the stone and said, *Thank you, Lord, for Mom and Dad and warming my heart with your love.*

Christmas Angel
by DeAnna Hambly

The moment John stepped onto the dock, his worries became real. He didn't like spending a week on the oil platform in the Gulf while his wife was at home alone, grieving the loss of their baby. But he had no choice. They both knew he had to work. On the rig, he could do nothing to help Marie. Now that he was on shore he had to do something, but what?

He spotted his faded red Toyota pickup halfway down the second isle. He tossed his hard hat onto the passenger seat and waited for the line of cars to exit the security gate. Tomorrow would be Christmas Eve. He couldn't think of a single gift that might make Marie smile. She was buried too deep in her depression, blaming herself for falling off the ladder while painting the nursery. The baby survived a few hours—long enough for John and Marie to hold her and say goodbye. After the funeral, Marie refused to leave the bedroom.

At the sound of a horn, John swerved to miss the oncoming car. "What am I going to do?" he shouted, as if someone far away might hear. He'd not been to church in years and wasn't sure if God would answer his prayers. But nothing else had worked. "God, I don't know how to help Marie. Can you please show me? Please God. I'm not asking for me. I'm asking for my wife."

As he passed the Wal-Mart, he noticed the sign: *Christmas Trees 50% Off.* Perfect. That would brighten up the house. He made a U-turn, pulled into the parking lot, and drove around until he found an open space. When he walked past the blue Chevy, a whimper drew his attention to the dog on the seat. He peered into the window and tapped the glass. "What's wrong little fellow?"

The sound of a woman clearing her throat startled John.

"And just what do you think *you're* doing, young man?" The woman's eyebrows were squeezed tightly together.

He stepped back from the car. "Oh, I was just talking to your dog." He reached to shake her hand. "I'm John Stelman."

"Doris." She dropped her bags onto the back seat.

"What kind of dog is he?"

"He is a *she.* A Fourche Terrier."

"She looks like Toto on *The Wizard of Oz.* Can I pet her?"

"Well she only bites strangers." She gently smiled. "Since the two of you have already introduced yourselves, I suppose it's okay."

She opened the car door and handed him the dog.

John stroked the dog's back. "She's cute. Do you know where I can find one like her?"

"I have two of her puppies left, a male and a

78

female." She pulled a business card from her purse. "If you want one, you need to come by my shop early tomorrow. It's Christmas Eve. They'll probably be gone by noon. The address is on the card."

John handed the dog back to Doris. "Thank you, Ma'am. I'll be there early."

At home, he grabbed the tree from the back of the pickup and hurried to unlock the door. He hoped to find Marie up and waiting, but the house was dark and silent, just as he had left it a week ago. He dropped his shoulders and leaned his back against the closed door. With a sigh, he stood the barren tree in the corner and turned on the light in the kitchen. A roach scurried out from the sink full of dirty dishes.

"Marie, I'm home." He gave the bedroom door a gentle push.

"I'm tired," she mumbled.

"Have you eaten today?"

She lifted the brown comforter and pulled it over her head. He turned the comforter back and kissed her forehead. "I've missed you. I bought us a Christmas tree. Will you help me decorate it?"

"I'm too tired."

The next morning, John decorated the tree, but he wasn't sure why. He had no hope, and he saw no reason to buy that puppy. But he told Doris he would be there, and he wasn't one to break a promise—not even to a stranger. He dressed and drove to Doris's shop.

Inside, the warm scent of holiday spices emanated from a burning candle. Doris came out from the back of the shop and dropped a forty-pound bag of dog food onto the floor. "I sold the male early this morning. If you want the female, you'd better grab her. A lady just called. She's supposed to come look at her this afternoon."

John had every intention of walking away empty-handed, but after holding the puppy, he didn't have the heart to say no. He was desperate, and he was willing to do anything to help Marie.

When he got the puppy home, he made a bed for her in the garage. "You'll have to stay out here 'til morning. I'll be back to check on you."

Early Christmas morning, he slipped from the bed and tied a red bow around the puppy's neck. He placed her on the bed beside Marie, then shouted, *"Merry Christmas!"* He turned to go to the kitchen but paused outside the doorway.

Marie rolled over and looked at the puppy, then slid under the comforter.

John snickered as the puppy tugged at the heavy comforter until she had exposed Marie's head.

"Stop it!" Marie said.

The puppy turned its head from side to side.

Marie glared at her. "Go away!"

The puppy lunged and licked her face.

John went to the kitchen and poured the coffee. He gathered pillows behind Marie and helped her sit up. "Here." He handed her the warm cup.

She sipped the coffee, and with a raspy voice asked, "Where'd you get that?"

"From a pet shop."

She looked puzzled. "What is it?"

John smiled. "She's a *Wizard of Oz* dog."

Marie laughed. "She looks like a wizard with all that hair. Have you fed her?"

"Not yet."

"Did you get dog food?"

"I left it in my truck. I'll go get it."

Marie slipped into her robe and picked up the puppy. "We better take you outside."

The puppy squatted briefly in the frost-covered grass.

"That's a *good* girl." Marie tucked the shaking puppy inside her warm robe and scurried inside.

John returned with the bag of dog food.

"Brrr...it's freezing out there." She patted the puppy's head. "I think I might like having you around. It gets pretty lonely with John out on the rig all week."

For a moment, she and John locked eyes. Then she turned to the sink and pushed her sleeves back. "Do you like the name Angel?"

He put his arm around her shoulder. "Yes. I love that name."

Marie looked down at the puppy curled beneath her feet. "Well then, I guess we'll call you Angel."

John kissed Marie on the cheek and reached for the puppy. He walked to the bedroom and knelt by the bed. Tears filled his eyes as he softly prayed, "Thank you God. Thank you for helping me find our Christmas Angel."

Doctor On Call
by Dee Dee Kellett

Mac touched the cold granite headstone: *Monica McGuire, Beloved Wife; Katie McGuire, Beloved Daughter; A Drunk Driver in a Swoon; Sent Them to Jesus Way Too Soon.* After three years of daily visits to the gravesite on his way home from the hospital, tears still filled his eyes. "I miss you so much," he whispered, as if he didn't want the trees to hear. "I'll see you soon."

He wasn't saying goodbye. He was saying hello. This was his closest connection to the family he had lost, a place where he didn't feel alone, where memories could bring a taste of the joys he once had, where his anger didn't consume his soul, where he could ask God *why*, which helped a little, even without any answers.

"I really am coming to see you," Mac said, feeling relieved. Monica and Katie had died on Christmas Eve. If he hadn't been on call at the hospital to see a patient, he would have been with them. Spending Christmas alone was a living hell. He'd rather be in Heaven. He was a doctor. A lethal injection was no problem. With access to the drugs that would put him to sleep, he would wake up at Heaven's gates. He decided against telling them his plan and walked away.

The next morning, even though it was Christmas Eve, Mac felt great as he walked into the hospital. All that bothered him was the lack of guarantees. Who was to say, if he took his own life, he wouldn't wind up in Hell, eternally separated from Monica and Katie? When he heard the preacher say rejecting life on Earth isn't the same as rejecting God, he felt sure his salvation was secure. A shadow of doubt bothered him at times, but not today. His thoughts focused on Monica and Katie, and walking with them on streets of transparent gold.

"You're late, doctor," the nurse said. "If you don't get to 307 soon, I may have to strangle the lady." She smiled like somebody who was only slightly serious. "Oh, and 305. She's new, brought up from pediatric ICU. Sorry, I haven't had time to update your chart. The holidays, you know."

Strange how so many doctors and nurses took sick during this season. They were always shorthanded on the holidays. Add the fact that, except for him, every person in the hospital would rather be at home. This was shaping up to be the most unusual of days.

Yes, it would be.

After knocking on the door, he walked into room 305. "Hello, I'm Doctor McGuire. You can call me Mac." When he went to shake her hand, he felt like he was touching Katie. They could have passed for sisters. Maybe nine years old. Blonde curls. Bright, intelligent eyes. About the same age as when Katie died. "What is your name?"

"Hannah Marie Thompson, but you can call me Hannah. I have chronic lymphocytic leukemia, but that's okay because Mom said God has a reason that he picked me to have this disease. It's not so bad except for the shots. I hate needles, but you get used to them." All that in a single breath. "I really like the friends I've made in the hospital. Some are very sick, so we might not see one another again until we get to Heaven."

"I see." Mac struggled with which would have been better—for Katie to be like Hannah, suffering from a terminal disease, or to be rushed off to Heaven by a drunk driver. This was the hardest part of his job, to see an innocent child suffering. He felt his face redden. How could a loving God allow kids to go through so much pain and then death?

"What's wrong, Doctor Mac?"

"What do you mean?"

"You look like my older brother when I took his iPod. Wow, did he ever get mad! His face turned red and he grabbed it out of my hand. He said bad words that Mom says make God mad. Did you have something stolen?"

Come to think of it, yes, a wife and daughter, a loss this youngster could never understand. "No," Mac said, "I don't have an older brother or sister. I'm all alone."

As she shifted on her bed, Hanna looked concerned, like she wanted to help a friend who was hurting. "Do you have any children?"

"No." He choked on the word and wanted to leave and regain his composure, but if it were Katie in the room, he would have to stay, so he stayed. "No," he said, "not anymore."

"I'm sorry." She paused, apparently wanting to say something more but not sure how to say it. "Did they go to be with Jesus?"

84

Why was he having this conversation? What was the point? Maybe it came from no longer being able to talk to his daughter. He pushed back the tears from his eyes. "My wife and daughter died in a car wreck on Christmas Eve, on their way home from Grandma's. I should have been with them, but I had to see patients here at the hospital. God could have stopped the drunken driver. If they had left five minutes later, the wreck wouldn't have happened." Anger rose in his throat. "When I see God, I want to know why he took them from me."

Hanna sniffled like she was on the verge of tears, then stiffened. "Mom says the ways of the Lord are not our ways. Complaining keeps us from being thankful, and Christmas is a time to be thankful. She says asking God to explain himself is like saying we're smarter than he is. God isn't required to give us answers, but we're required to trust him. That's what Mom says."

"You have a smart mom, and you're pretty smart yourself, young lady." Mac felt like asking the girl to pray for him. God knows, he needed it. He didn't ask. He felt like he should pray for the girl, but he didn't do that either. What he did do is silently ask God's forgiveness for not trusting him.

He decided, after work, he would take a poinsettia and Christmas decorations to the cemetery. There he would thank God for the gift of his Son, who had shown him peace and joy in the midst of suffering. He would thank God for the years with Monica and Katie and for the assurance that he would one day see them again. And he thanked God for the privilege of helping others who were hurting, because he understood what hurting felt like.

Breakdown
by Lori Freeland

When Kelly turned off the ignition and looked across the grocery store parking lot, she froze. Was that Dad's green Ford pickup? No, it couldn't be, but the mere thought that it might be, made her want to get away. What would she do if he saw her?

A man bundled in a green hunting jacket was leaning under the raised hood, about the same height as Dad, but thinner. The sight of him put a bitter taste in her mouth from the pancakes she had eaten on Christmas Eve, ten years ago. She remembered the sweet smell of hot maple syrup and the unexplainable silence before Dad blurted the words that broke her heart: *I'm moving in with Susan.* He never looked up, but continued to cut his pancakes into neat little squares.

It couldn't be his truck. Why would he be 350 miles from home on Christmas Eve, at the grocery store near her house? He didn't even know she lived here. Or that she was married and had two kids.

An SUV rolled by, illuminating Indiana plates and an American flag painted on the back window. *This can't be happening to me.* She wiped away the frost on her window. Why was he still driving—or trying to drive—that old beaten-up truck?

Snowflakes splattered the windshield, making it hard to see. She couldn't sit there forever, or she would have to get out of the car and chip off the ice. He was sure to see her then. She turned the key in the ignition and flipped on the wipers, moving away the snow in wet chunks. If only it were that easy to wipe away the past. Why hadn't she just skipped the glaze for the ham and stayed home? The kids wouldn't have noticed. Jake would eat anything.

Dad slammed the hood and pulled a cell phone from his pocket. His hair had grayed almost to the whiteness of the snow. He was definitely Dad, still with his bushy mustache. He played with his phone for a minute, then closed it and slumped against the fender.

Kelly knew what she should do. If it had been a neighbor, she wouldn't have hesitated to get out and see what she could do to help. Dad was a different matter. She vowed never to forgive him, and she hadn't.

Last-minute shoppers avoided him. *Please*, she begged. *Someone out there, help him.* She rubbed the fingers of her gloves to eliminate the tingling. This was not *her* problem. Dad was the one who walked away—ten years ago to the day. Others should help him, people whose Christmas hadn't been ruined by him.

That day when he finally looked up from his pancakes, he had said, "You're all grown up. You don't need me," as if that should be sufficient explanation. She was all of sixteen—hardly grown up at all.

Dad stood, looked around, then sagged against the truck, head in his hands. Why didn't he go inside and ask for help? Was he so old that he didn't know what to do? Eventually he would figure it out. *Just leave*, she told herself. Why couldn't she forget she ever saw him and go home? He had certainly forgotten about her.

With a groan, she got out of the car and kicked the door shut. Painful needles shot through her toes. She trudged across the snow to his truck and cleared her throat.

Dad looked up, his eyes wide with surprise. "Kelly! I didn't expect... I mean I was... I was coming to..." His voice trailed off as he took a long look at her. "Baby, you're all grown up."

"What do you expect after ten years?" She thrust her cell forward. "Would you like to use my cell phone?"

He kept his hands at his side. "I was bringing dinner to your house. Mom gave me your address. She showed me pictures of your kids—my grandchildren."

"You never talk to Mom." She took a step back. "Why aren't you with your own family on Christmas Eve? Or are you starting over for the third time?"

He pulled his coat tighter and watched the snow collect on the sleeve. "Can we go somewhere warmer where we can talk?"

"Why? What's left to say? You said it was over ten years ago. It still is."

"I apologized to your mom." He stuffed his gloved hands into his coat pockets. "I'd like to apologize to you."

Kelly stiffened. She felt her face redden, and not from the cold. "I don't think so."

"Please." Moisture shone in his eyes, and his begging tone was pitiful.

Geez, the last time she'd seen him cry was his father's funeral fifteen years ago. "As soon as I get glaze for the ham, I'm headed home."

"No need to go in," he said. "Mom always glazed the ham, so I figured you would too. You can take my grocery sacks, with another ham and plenty of glaze." He looked so sad, yet his tone indicated he would be satisfied if she would just take his groceries home—like that was enough to feel like he was in touch with the family he used to have.

Kelly kicked a chunk of ice. "Fine, I'll take the groceries." She thrust out her phone again. "Here, call your buddy down at the garage. I'll drop you off at a hotel."

After phoning the garage and making arrangements, he left the keys under the floor mat and grabbed the grocery bags off the seat.

On the first turn out of the parking lot, Kelly said, "Okay, we can stop at a restaurant so you can apologize. I can't stay long. I need to get home." She sighed in silent regret when she realized the only place open this late on Christmas Eve was the IHOP. She had sworn off eating pancakes ten years ago and didn't look forward to seeing them on anybody's plate.

A wearied waitress handed them a menu. "The pancake breakfast is on special—"

Of course it is. Kelly put her hand up. "Just coffee, please."

Dad ordered coffee too and waited for the waitress to fill their cups. "If I could do it all over"—he paused to regain his composure—"I would never have left." A tear rolled down his cheek. "It wasn't right, what I did. You were my daughter." He reached across the table, his palm up. "You still are."

She tucked her hair behind her ear. Why was this so hard when she'd waited so long for him to be sorry? Did he expect her to let go of ten years of anger in a single moment? Impossible.

He let out a deep breath. "I've missed you for ten years, and the pain gets worse every Christmas."

Kelly had to admit that her own bitterness had been a long-time source of pain. Could she accept his apology when what he did was so wrong? "Okay." She laid her hand on his. "We'll talk. That's all I can give you."

Dad broke down and cried. "That's enough— more than enough for today."

The Real Meaning of Christmas
by Janet White

My five-year-old daughter, Jadyn, shrieked with joy when I told her we could leave the dinner table. By having to wait, the joyful anticipation of opening presents would be even greater, and I intended to get the most from this moment.

Jadyn and my niece ran into the living room and plopped down next to the towering pile of gifts. I scooted them away and sat beside them. "Be quiet now, so Poppy can read the Christmas story." We had a tradition that needed to be followed.

Knowing the words by heart, I looked to see how others were enjoying this time. Mom sat in her recliner with that appreciative grin when the family surrounded her. My brother and sister-in-law were holding hands on the couch, thrilled to be expecting their second child. Randy, my husband, leaned back and gave me his half-crooked grin that said, *I'm glad I married you.* After eight years, his expression still made my heart skip a beat.

As soon as Dad finished reading, I had to quiet the

girls. "We can't open presents yet. Each of us has to tell what we're thankful for this year."

Randy never liked this part. He wanted to let the kids open their presents, but we had a tradition and I wouldn't let it go. When his turn came, he smiled at me and said, "I'm thankful to have Janet and Jadyn. And for our families." He hesitated, like he thought he might choke on the words he was about to say. "This year, I'm also thankful for Janet's health."

How'd I get so lucky?

I thought I was going to cry, so I turned to face the rest of the family and swallowed hard. It was my turn to speak. "I'm thankful for all of you. For my health. Most of all, I'm thankful for an awesome husband. Randy was my rock when we found out I had breast cancer."

Through bi-lateral mastectomies, my self-esteem never took a hit. I had Randy to thank for that. I remembered what he said to me: *Janet, you and I will be the only ones who will ever see the scars. I don't care what you look like. I just want to keep you around so we can grow old together.*

Tears filled my eyes.

My Christmas list was very small compared to all the reasons I had to be thankful. I was abundantly blessed. Only God knew how my life could get any better.

Four months later, the phone rang.

Silence. "Janet…" The voice of Randy's police chief. "There was a high-speed chase that ended in a wreck," he said. Another pause. "Janet, Randy didn't make it."

Sudden shock.

Months of grieving.

A struggle to fill the void in Jadyn's life.

In November, I was trying not to think about the holidays.

As I drove with Jadyn to The Warm Place, our grief-counseling center, I remembered what Randy had said last Christmas. I heard the broken voice of Randy's police chief on the phone: *Randy didn't make it.* Our Christmas tradition would never be the same. How could I make it through the day? I wiped away my tears.

Holding my hand, Jadyn chattered away as she practically dragged me up the sidewalk. Her eyes sparkled every time we entered the old house. This was the only place she felt normal, because every other kid had lost a parent too. As soon as the door opened, Jadyn ran off to her group.

Emotionally exhausted, I wandered into the adult room and sat by the fireplace.

The group leader gave her usual, understanding smile. "Write down what is worrying you about the coming holidays," she said.

That was easy. I scrawled: *How to be thankful.*

When my turn came, I read my words aloud. Slowly. With hesitation, like this was a secret I shouldn't tell.

"Maybe it's because of my faith," one lady said, "but it helps me to think of at least one thing every day that I'm thankful for."

Why had I struggled with my words? *How to be thankful.* For the past seven months, I had done my best to focus on the good things. Maybe I needed to change my view of the "what are you thankful for" question. Maybe I should ask how to be thankful instead.

The next Sunday morning, I sat on a red-cushioned pew. Of all things, we were singing hymns of thanksgiving. When the music stopped, the leader said, "Does anybody feel led to stand and tell what they are thankful for?"

Who, me? I glanced up at the ceiling.

Seriously, God, do I have to do this now?

I sensed God pushing me to put into practice what he had been teaching me. With a huge lump in my throat, I stood and said, "I'm thankful for the support of my family and friends these last seven months." When I sat down, I felt like a heavy weight had been lifted off my shoulders.

Later, the missions director asked if I would say something at our community Thanksgiving dinner. I glanced at my dad, not believing I was saying yes.

"I knew you'd be asked," Dad said. "I've already started praying."

At the dinner, I shared with a shaky voice what God had taught me about being thankful. "God doesn't expect me to be thankful for the bad things in my life," I said. "He isn't this egotistical guy waiting for me to thank him, just to feed his ego. No, he wants me to focus on the good things because that's best for me."

I breathed a sigh of relief, thankful I hadn't fallen apart.

At home, exhausted and emotionally drained, I cried uncontrollably. *If Thanksgiving takes this much out of me, how am I going to make it through Christmas?* Then, like light from Heaven, another thought: *Adjust your perspective. Focus on the real meaning of Christmas.*

For thirty-two years, the holiday celebration had been a family tradition centered on having fun, giving and getting presents, and enjoying the pretty lights and decorations.

My excitement had never been focused on the birth of our Savior, how he came to live a sinless life, was crucified for our sake and rose from the dead. We could be forgiven and live forever with him.

At that moment, I knew what it would be like at Christmas, when we sat in a circle without Randy, and I had to say why I was thankful. I would say, *Because of the baby Jesus, I will see Randy again. He'll be waiting for me when I walk through the pearly gates. I'll run into his arms for a big bear hug. Then he'll show me around Heaven's transparent streets of gold.*

I was thankful beyond words because I had discovered the real meaning of Christmas.

Santa Buster
by Suzanne Hearn

I thought about shooting him. If I had a hit list, I wouldn't need to check it twice to know Santa's name was on it.

I imagined what the scene in the shopping mall would be like. In the foreground, red-faced, tear-drenched youngsters were gathered beneath the North Pole sign, a mixture of anger and grief painfully evident. In front of them stood the tombstone.

HERE LIES SANTA CLAUS
ALIAS, CHRISTMAS THIEF
HE SHOWED UP AGAIN
AND SHE DONE HIM IN

It was a shameful but strangely satisfying image. Heaven help me. I couldn't really do it. There would only be more Santas. And there were the children to consider.

Every Thanksgiving, Santa never failed to show up.

It went like this: Tummy still tight with turkey and dressing. Dishes stacked to the ceiling. I plopped onto

96

the couch and propped up my feet for some TV and pie. Then it happened—the first Santa sighting. I thought, *It's the month before Christmas when Santa arrives. My ulcer comes back, and I break out in hives.* He was all ho-ho-ho and I was all no-no-no. *Please not again!* I wanted to heave my pie straight at the screen, but that wouldn't help. I'd have to clean up the mess.

One by one, year after year, the Santas came, a steady stream of red velour and flowing white beards. The inevitable gift-giving game arrived, and I had no choice but to succumb to the commercialization. Santa represented all the exhausting seasonal tasks I dreaded at Christmas.

Don't fight this. Conserve energy. Breathe.

I set down my pie and picked up my purse. Mall time again. My unstated plan was to take the high road. Avoid the jolly beast. Keep my distance so our eyes could never meet. Surely there was a shred of redemption in my distaste for him. I could be content if we never met face-to-face. Not ever.

As a kid, I had squirmed in his lap many times, at first crying, then learning to beg for gifts. I played the game until I figured out the catch and called it quits. When I was in junior high, Mom made me sit on his lap for a picture with my baby cousin. I crossed my arms, clung to my purse, and tried not to touch him with anything but my backside. Who was this guy, anyway? I was mortified. Maybe my adulthood angst about Santa had been born in that moment. Regardless, I had long since lost the warm, fuzzy feelings that fueled sentimental fires.

As an adult, I viewed Santa as nothing but a list of chores and the enemy of peace and prosperity. I considered counseling, but preferred my imaginary gun, always cocked and ready to take aim at the crafty Christmas kidnapper. If a face-to-face moment ever came, I would be ready to take on the big boy.

On a rainy afternoon, I went to a mini-museum where an exhibit chronicled the history of a popular department store owned by my friend Monty's family. Heartwarming memorabilia filled the room. I rounded the corner and there Santa was, chatting nonchalantly with Monty.

For a split second, Santa's presence in such pictur-esque surroundings spilled nostalgic warmth my way. But years of target practice brought me back to my senses. *Focus*. I was mentally armed, dangerous, and at close range.

"Suzanne," Monty said with a tone of delight, "meet a friend of mine, his name is—"

Whoa, hold on. No names please. Nothing personal. Don't make this harder than it has to be. Better that the victim remain nameless behind that white mass of hair and fur. *Wink at me with either eye, buster, and I'll only take a second to blacken the other one.* I kept my clenched fist in my pock-et, a tiny but powerful concealed weapon. This was it, my moment of truth.

"Well, hello," I said with a constrained smile. "I've wanted to shoot you for a long time." The words blurt-ed out like a confession burning to be voiced.

"Sure." He glanced at my bulging side pocket. "Is that your camera?"

"Huh? Oh, yeah." Quickly I tried to gather my thoughts. "I'll take my shot in a second, but first a couple of questions."

"Fire away."

Oh, God, help me. "Why, uh… I mean, how did you… What makes you—"

"Enjoy being Santa?" His cheeks turned rosy and he had a gleam in his eye.

I didn't hear what he said after that. His unmistakable resemblance to the Santa of my childhood and the smell of popcorn took me back to long-forgotten memories. He fit the picture so perfectly. Wait. What was Santa saying to me? He again had my attention.

"My father was the maintenance man at Monty's department store," he said. "His first love was the Lord, then us kids, and next, Christmas. When the old store Santa retired, he snatched up the job, thinking of the fun and the extra cash. The Lord has a way of changing hearts."

He stroked his beard, raised a brow, and smiled warmly. "One Saturday afternoon, with a child on his lap and a waiting line of young-uns as long as Texas, Dad felt a tweak in his heart. In his own way, he experienced the words of Jesus: 'Let the little children come to me.' He always said true believers have Jesus living inside, and we all need to be on the lookout for opportunities to spill him out on others."

Santa sighed, leaned back, and patted his stomach. "After the kids recited their lists, he gave them real gifts. Over time, he found clever ways to share God's word. He never let a child off his lap without whispering a truth and a blessing, asking God to give them the desires of their hearts."

He straightened up and winked. "But you asked about me. My Santa gig is different. My baby brother was deaf, so I learned sign language. It's become my secret Santa weapon. I'm only here today as a favor to

Monty. I'm usually suited up at the deaf school. Just like dad, I deliver all sorts of quiet messages. Did you know you can shout for joy in sign language? Their little worlds can be pretty silent."

Packaged in velour and fur, fitted with a jumbo red hat and a heart to match, here stood a real Santa.

Deep in my heart there arose such a flutter, all of my anger had melted like butter.

"Well," he said. "Are you ready to shoot me?" He glanced at my bulging pocket.

"Sure." I turned and pulled out my camera from the other pocket, looking toward the people gathered nearby. "Would someone please shoot Santa and me? I want the perfect Christmas shot."

For the first shot, I aimed my camera at him while he made joyful signs with his hands. Then we stood together as the flash of the camera hit us both between the eyes.

His name was Buster, and that blew me away.

Apple E-Bay
by Barbara Brooks

As the holidays approached, I was grieving over the loss of Iris, our English Setter companion for fourteen years.

My husband, Larry, sat on the couch, staring into space. "I miss her," he said.

"Me too." Without a loving whimper or the swish of her tail, the house felt as quiet as a funeral home. I wiped a tear from my eye. I imagined Iris at the back door, her tail wagging to greet us as soon as she heard the garage door open. "Coming home won't feel the same."

"What do you want to do?"

I wanted to sit and cry. Iris had been like a daughter to me. Ronald Reagan once said the best way to get over a dog's death was to get another one soon. Larry left the house with car keys in hand and a determined look in his eyes. I feared what he might bring home. No dog could take Iris's place.

After two hours, I stared at my watch. What was taking so long? Finally, he walked in, looking radiant, carrying a package. "I haven't visited a pet store for fourteen years. I told the clerk we just lost our dog, and I wanted to get you another pet so you won't be so lonely."

I laughed. "You just said that so you wouldn't look like some pet-loving sissy."

"We wandered up and down the aisles. I barely glanced at the caged lizards, gerbils, parakeets, pups, and kittens. I wasn't interested in the clerk's sales pitches until I spotted the perfect pet. I raced toward the cage hoping nobody would get there before I did."

"And what was so great about this pet?"

"The clerk said she is festive, both literally and figuratively. Her stature is small, but she exudes enormous character. She's not afraid of anything and protects her territory like a guard dog."

Like a guard dog? Apparently she wasn't a dog. "Is she friendly?"

"She loves giving kisses and enjoys gentle rubbing behind the ears. She greets customers with vigor but hates to say goodbye to new acquaintances. The clerk mentioned a couple of things we should know—to help with the bonding process. She likes to hear that she's pretty. She thrives on attention and shows it by strutting around like a queen. Her favorite color is purple and she prefers food to be served in variations of that shade."

"Oh, that's good to know." I wasn't sharing Larry's enthusiasm.

"She also does some mischievous things you should know about."

"Like what?"

"She can be cantankerous. When reprimanded,

she'll react. However, once she grows attached to you, she'll love you for life."

I peeked through the air holes of the cardboard carrier and whatever was inside squawked at me. "What is that?"

Larry looked as proud as a kid who had won first prize at the country fair. "That's Peanut. She's a double yellow-headed Amazon parrot."

"This bird has an attitude." I wasn't pleased. "A parakeet wouldn't bite off my finger."

"But a parrot will outlive us. We won't be grieving over her loss."

He was right. I didn't want to grieve over another pet. He was being a thoughtful husband, and I was content with a parrot as long as she remained Larry's responsibility. He was the bird lover, not me.

On Monday morning, Larry came into the kitchen with a longing look that said I was in trouble. "Since I have to fly to Denver today, would you step in and nurture Peanut in my absence?"

I sighed. We both knew I had no choice. "I have no idea what to do, but I'll figure it out."

I couldn't kill a bird that cost more than my cashmere sweater. I leafed through Larry's book on the proper care and feeding of parrots. Standing next to her cage, I pointed to the book. "Wow, Peanut, it says you can mimic words easier if they are repeated."

"Wow," the parrot said in perfect English.

"Did you understand what I just said?"

She shrugged like she didn't need me to tell her what to do. After hearing my words, she repeated the ones she liked, but not in the same order and only when she wanted to say them.

I decided to teach Peanut a few holiday phrases so she could greet visitors with some Christmas cheer. I pulled a kitchen chair close to the cage and sat down. "Happy Holidays," I said, followed by, "Merry Christmas." I repeated the phrases over and over.

No response. She looked at me as if I were speaking a foreign language.

Exasperated, I said, "Bite me," and walked away.

Our son, Jim, his fiancé, and her mother were coming for a visit, and I wanted Peanut to make a good first impression. "Peanut," I said, "please say your lines when our company gets here."

"Whatever," she said.

Larry and I decorated the house with garland, snow globes, and stockings. The Christmas season was the perfect time for friends to visit us and dote on Peanut. She loved the attention and flirted without inhibition. I hung Christmas bells in her cage, which she rang constantly. I envisioned them as servant bells chiming, "Come feed me. Come give me attention."

Peanut was definitely in the holiday spirit. I kept trying to get her to recite the holiday greetings. She tried, but her "happy holidays" came out garbled, sounding like "apple e-bay." At least she was making an effort.

I looked at her with confidence and spoke in an encouraging tone. "You'll get it right when our guests are here."

Our company arrived mid-afternoon on Christmas Eve. Larry greeted them at the door and helped with their bags while I finished placing the last strands of tinsel on the tree.

"We're eager to meet Peanut," our future

daughter-in-law said.

"Hello," chirped a voice from the kitchen.

"Hi, Mom," my son said.

I walked up to give him a hug "I wasn't the one who said "hello." That was Peanut. Her cage is in the kitchen."

After we had greeted one other and visited for a moment, I took our guests to meet Peanut. She showed off her beautiful rainbow tail feathers and paraded on her perch like she was the main attraction at the circus.

Jim's future mother-in-law leaned toward the cage. "Oh, what a beautiful bird."

"Bite me," Peanut said.

My mouth dropped open. Larry gasped and coughed nervously.

"What did she say?"

I didn't know how to answer and looked to Larry for help.

Larry was staring at the bird in horror. Shaking his head, he turned to our guests. "We just have to stop letting her watch television."

"Apple e-bay," Peanut said.

And she was right. It was a happy holiday.

A Place for Jesus
by Barbara Hollis

JoAnna's hands trembled as she read the notice again. *Three (3) Day Notice to Pay Rent or Quit.* This was day four. There was no need to wait for a Writ of Possession from the court. With no husband, no friends, no car, and no money to pay rent, she and her three-year-old daughter, Kate, were out in the cold—literally. Where could she go?

"Kate, we have to leave," JoAnna said with tears in her eyes. "Come get your coat on."

"Can Jesus come?" Kate wrapped the white blanket around her baby doll and held it tightly.

"Yes, but you'll have to carry him. There isn't any room in the suitcase."

JoAnna grasped her daughter's arm that was wrapped around her baby Jesus. With her other hand she pulled their suitcase down the snow-covered sidewalk toward the business district.

As soon as Kate saw the golden arches, she begged for a Happy Meal.

"I'm sorry, honey, we need to get to the mission

before the kitchen closes." It didn't matter that Christmas was just two days away. JoAnna couldn't afford the cost of a child's meal and free toy.

When they were about to pass McDonald's, Kate pulled on JoAnna's coat. "I need to go potty." Powerful words, coming from the mouth of a three-year-old. This was no place for a little one to have an accident, and the mission was still half a mile away.

"Okay," JoAnna said, but just for a minute to go to the bathroom. We can't stay." On the way back outside, she said, "Look, I think it's starting to snow. Isn't it pretty?"

Kate looked the opposite way, toward the children's play area. "Slide," she cried. "Want to slide."

JoAnna had to pick up screaming Kate and carry her. Kate didn't quit crying until they turned the corner and the arches were out of sight. "See, baby Jesus isn't crying. Are you hungry?" JoAnna was the one about ready to cry. The mission would fill their stomachs with soup and crackers, but where would they spend the night? The wind was stronger now, and the snow was falling steadily.

In the mission, JoAnna chose the seats at the table near the door. The far side of the room was warmer, but the homeless who were gathered there smelled like they hadn't had a bath since Christmas a year ago. She held the steaming bowl of soup near her mouth so she could breathe-in the warmth and pleasant aroma. How long would it be before she too was among the homeless, wearing tattered rags? While JoAnna slurped soup from her spoon, Kate filled her belly with crackers.

JoAnna turned to the bearded man, who was wiping clean the plaid-oilcloth-covered table next to her.

"Where's Irene?"

The man never looked up. "Got the day off. She should be back tomorrow."

JoAnna sighed. She didn't know the name of anybody else to ask about a place to stay.

Kate looked at JoAnna, then the man. "My baby Jesus needs a bed tonight."

The man smiled at them like a waiter ready to take their order. "Ma'am, if you're needin' a place to bed for the night, you might check with the manager at the Community Storehouse down the street."

The manager of the Storehouse wasn't in. "He won't be back until tomorrow," the lady at the counter said. "He owns a big company and is often gone on business."

"Oh... well, thank you anyway." JoAnna was out of options. It was Christmas, a season for gifts and generosity. She had always been willing to help others, but she didn't know how to beg. Who could she see? What would she say?

They couldn't sleep outside. They would freeze to death. She could come back tomorrow and see the manager, but first they had to survive the night. Only one possibility existed, and it wasn't a good one—the old train caboose on the edge of town that served as a novelty welcome sign for travelers. If the door wasn't locked or rusted shut, she and Kate might snuggle up tight in one corner.

Did she dare take her little girl on such a journey? The snow hadn't stopped, and it was getting colder. The walk past McDonalds had been tough enough, but another mile to the outskirts of town? Could they make it? What if they couldn't get into the caboose? They might freeze to death before they could find an open door to a barn somewhere.

Kate looked up at the lady behind the counter. "My baby Jesus needs a bed tonight."

"He does, does he?" The lady smiled like a teacher who was greeting a new kindergarten student. "We have toys and blankets, but I don't think we have a bed in his size."

"I'm sorry," JoAnna said, "I don't know your name. You'll have to excuse my daughter."

"My name is Florence. Florence Johnson."

JoAnna's lip quivered and tears filled her eyes. "Six months ago, my husband drove away and I haven't heard from him since. I've looked for a job, but it's tough when you have a three-year-old at home. With food stamps, we've survived, but I couldn't pay the rent. I don't know where we're going to sleep tonight."

"For just one night, you could probably stay at my place. But I should check with my husband first."

"No, you don't need to do that. I was thinking about that caboose on the edge of town. I don't know if the door will open, but if you wouldn't mind driving us there and could loan us a few blankets—"

"Girl, you'll freeze out there. Do you know how cold it's supposed to be tonight? If you don't mind the hard floor, we can spread out some blankets to make a thick pad back in the warehouse. Would that be okay?"

"Can my baby Jesus have a bed?" Kate's face gleamed with excitement.

The next morning, Florence introduced JoAnna to the manager. He obviously wanted to help, but JoAnna had no work experience that would qualify her for anything above minimum wage. That wasn't enough to pay for an apartment and day care.

Kate didn't appear to be listening. She was in the toys section in the next aisle, playing. "Do you like your bed, Jesus?" she asked her baby.

The manager looked at Kate and smiled. "I can think of one possibility. It's not much, but if you worked hard, it might develop into a valuable position. I can't make any promises though."

"What is it?"

"My company is opening a day care for its employees. If you went to work there, you could bring your daughter." He glanced toward Kate and smiled. "And we could make a place for Jesus."

Christmas Building
by Gail Newman

I drummed my fingers against the steering wheel, waiting for the traffic light to change. Two cars moved forward. Waiting again. I checked my watch, wondering if I would make it to work on time. Maybe not.

On the next cycle, two cars sped through the intersection on red, proof that none of us wanted to watch our reflections in the bank building glass. Songs of snow and sleigh bells on the radio reminded me of parties to attend and shopping yet to be done. This was one season when nobody had time to waste. I wanted to say a few choice words about the delay, but didn't. After all, it was the season to be jolly. I smiled and tried to be content with conditions I couldn't change. What was wrong with the traffic?

When the next few cars moved forward, I expected to see my favorite building with its peeling paint and faded brick, a classic reminder of the good old days. Oh, no! Only half the building was still standing. Crash! A bulldozer pushed down a wall while a front end loader dropped debris into the truck. A tear came to my eye.

I didn't know whether to be angry or hurt, so I chose both emotions. What right did men have to tear the building down? At five stories, it was once the skyscraper in town, but years of progress had made it an unsightly dwarf. Not to me. I was losing my best friend.

Many seasons had come and gone. Winter was my favorite time, when the snow fell and strings of red and green lights made the building a perfect picture for a postcard. I remembered the night I was sitting at this intersection, headed to a Christmas party with friends. The rooms inside the building were brightly lit, and the blinds were pulled back. Faded gray metal desks were cluttered with papers. Bookshelves were in disarray, and the blackboard hadn't been cleaned in a month. Waste-paper baskets overflowed with trash.

The view of the inside was nothing like what I saw every day from the street. I wondered, *Was I like that building—beautiful to people passing by, but not looking so good on the inside?* I would never want to open the dirty closet of my heart or reveal the clutter in my back rooms.

Did I look okay for the party? I flipped on the light and stared at the rear-view mirror. Yes, all my time at the beauty shop hadn't been wasted.

I was like that building, wanting to look good.

Appearances were important, but that wasn't the only concern I needed to have. God knew my heart. Both he and I knew places that weren't as clean and straight as we wanted. In a whisper I echoed the words of David, *Wash me, and make me white as snow.* I didn't want to wait until spring for deep cleaning. From that moment on, I felt a need to be as presentable within myself as what I wanted people to see on the outside.

The next day, I went to the shopping mall with a different attitude, looking for just the right gifts for family and friends. My focus shifted from what they would think of me to what I knew would please them. The name from the Angel Tree let me do something special for a needy child. My Christmas cards carried exactly the right message to reveal God's love. I wanted people to be encouraged and find hope because they knew I cared, especially in a season when our hearts should be filled with joy because of his gifts.

For years, that building on the corner had stood as an icon for my changed life. It was a daily source of inspiration that made me want to keep showing God's love. Now it was gone with no notice. No chance to say goodbye. No time to adjust. What would I do now?

The light changed to green, and I drove by the sign announcing the construction of a new Italian restaurant. What would the corner look like after the construction was complete? A neon sign. Strings of colored lights. Plenty of space for parking, and an invitation for great food. The thought made me hungry.

Food. That was something the old building never had to offer. Is that what I wanted to become— someone who fed others spiritually?

Something good was being torn down so something even better could rise in its place. I drove to work with a new attitude. I set aside my anger and hurt and filled my heart with joy for the opportunity we have to feed the hungry. That new building would be a constant reminder of God's purpose that I had just discovered for my life.

Yes, this Christmas would be another wonderful season of building.

Celebrity Christmas
by Mary Ellen O'Gorman

I was merely a nurse on assignment when I was asked to care for Buddy Fogelson at Presbyterian Hospital in Dallas. While lying sick in bed, both rich and poor people dress the same, and they have equally loud groans when they are in pain. Until his beautiful wife walked in, I only knew about his gall bladder problem. I didn't know he had made a fortune as a wildcatter in the oil industry and was married to movie star Greer Garson.

Every day, people called Buddy for market updates. He looked at me and shook his head like I would be smart to listen to him. He seemed to be waiting for the market to start moving up. "Mary Ellen," he said, "don't buy oil unless it gets over eighteen dollars a barrel."

When it was time for him to leave the hospital, Buddy and Greer asked if I would go home with them and be his fulltime caregiver while he battled Parkinson's disease. What made me so special? Was it my smile, or my tender touch? Maybe my fiery red hair

114

made people think I could be Greer's sister. Celebrities who don't lack for money can be terribly demanding and impossible to please. They were asking me to be part of their family, but I wasn't sure that was possible. I had never seen a penthouse, let alone lived in one.

A successful nurse has to know the patient's needs and take care of them. She can't sit idly by and wait for a call. How was I doing? I wasn't getting any complaints, but that can be true for people who are about to be fired. I wasn't sure how much longer they would want me, until I was asked if I could travel with them. What a wonderful gift before Christmas.

In Los Angeles, a whirlwind of activities surrounded me with the glitz and glitter of the movie star world. Except for watching Buddy's medication and sending reports to his doctor, I could be awed by the celebrities who came to their condo on Wilshire Boulevard. I felt like a superhero when I answered the phone and took messages from stars like Angela Lansbury and Van Johnson. When Van asked if I was a redhead and thought I was somebody he should know, my heart skipped a beat.

I went everywhere with Buddy and Greer, but I never dressed as a nurse. Buddy didn't want people to know how sick he was. At one fancy affair, I danced with Bob Hope. If this was Heaven, I was ready to go.

Greer and I were both bottle redheads. Twice, she was sick and couldn't go to an event, so she asked me to go in her place, dressed in her clothes. I worked hard to maintain self-control and not be awed by the celebrities in attendance. "Just be nice and don't say anything," she said, "and they won't know the difference." It worked. Nobody questioned my identity, so I was a star among a universe of stars.

One evening when we gathered at the table for dinner, Buddy handed envelopes to the staff, each one containing $3,000.00, because his horse, Ach Ack, had won his race. Buddy wanted to share the purse with his employees. The horse was named US Horse of the Year in 1971 and, after retirement, went on to sire forty stakes winners.

Greer and Buddy loved the horse races, so we often went to the track. Greer had a system. She bet only on the horse with the longest tail or the jockey who wore purple. I never knew what our winnings were. I just knew we were having fun. Any system achieving that goal was a good one.

On Christmas Eve we exchanged gifts at dinner. Greer gave Buddy a pair of socks, and he gave her a box of candy, which was a nice way to recognize that having each other was all they really needed. For my Christmas, I hoped for a little recognition but not much more. A nurse whose care is motivated by money should find a different profession. Their token of appreciation was a trip to Hawaii and $1,200.00 in spending money. This was one of those rare times when I didn't know what to say.

While Buddy was in the hospital for tests and gallbladder surgery, I enjoyed all the island tours. I wanted to see everything. At 1:30 in the morning, I trekked up the mountain just to see the sun rise. The climb was as cold as Arctic ice, but was well worth the effort. Like the dawn on the first day of creation, the horizon's spectacular burst of light left me breathless. The gold, pink, and lavender shades were so brilliant, I wanted to reach out and touch the clouds to be sure I wasn't dreaming.

In the four years I lived with Buddy and Greer, I saw their hopes and dreams and goals that sometimes ended in disappointment. They had fears, flaws, and insecurities that weren't much different from the average person who walks down the street. Their money didn't make them special. Their giving did.

They made Christmas a special season for me because they showed me so many ways to give.

Should Christmas Make Cents?
by Billy Cuchens

I had no one to blame but myself for choosing a profession where the voices of Burl Ives and Eartha Kitt played for ten hours a day. Had it not been for my dread of the season, I would have thanked my company for waiting until the day after Thanksgiving to play nonstop Christmas music. By the end of the first week of December, I was ready to take box cutters and go to work on the overhead speakers.

I wished Christmas could be something more than shopping, entertainment, and gift exchange.

Home late from work, I hadn't been plopped down on the couch for much more than a minute before my wife, Laurie, asked, "How was your day?"

Nothing was new, so what could I say? I forced a smile. "I spent all day listening to requests like *I need ten $5 gift cards and five $10 gift cards.*"

She gave me an understanding look, as if she could know how stressful my day had been. Then, she asked me to wake up early and take her shopping.

I shouldn't have smiled.

I had to ask myself, *Why do I work in retail?* Oh, yeah. I stumbled into it the same way most people did—I wasn't good at anything else, and I had a family to support. This was why I had so little money, why I was warming myself with a heavy bathrobe rather than turning up the heat, and why I was watching local channels instead of cable.

I flipped the channel, looking for something upbeat, something to end my day on a more positive note. What was I expecting? Sympathy? I might have gotten that a few days earlier when *A Charlie Brown Christmas* came on. Charlie Brown asked if anyone could tell him the true meaning of Christmas. I couldn't get that line out of my head. The idea that I wasn't the only one who was a little down during this season didn't comfort me. Rather, I thought about when the show originally aired.

I said to Laurie, "You know, nothing has changed in fifty years. Nobody knows the true meaning of Christmas." She called me a "Scrooge," and I thought about the countless remakes of *A Christmas Carol*. No matter whether it was the version starring Fred Flintstone or *Star Trek's* Jean-Luc Picard, I was put off by the story's climax. The old curmudgeon runs amuck through the city, buying things for the people who were nice to him an hour ago. I couldn't help but wonder what that had to do with the birth of Jesus.

I flipped to another channel. *It's a Wonderful Life* was on. I didn't mind when it was shown without commercials, which clocked in at just over two hours. But the network television version began at seven p.m. and concluded just before sunrise. At eight o'clock, George finally met Mary. At nine, George was slapping

119

around his drunken uncle. At ten, he was in a bar praying and getting punched in the face. By eleven, he was finally jumping off the bridge. At that point, I was so despondent that I found myself wishing Clarence would mind his own business and let George drown.

What did this film have to do with Christmas? It was about one man's downward spiral and subsequent realization that his life had significance. The message was rewarding enough, despite the fact that George's decline takes 90 percent of the film. But that's not what bothered me. I couldn't see what the story had to do with the birth of Jesus. Where was the angel announcing God's plan to save the world and bring peace and goodwill to men? Evidently, when the climax of a film just happens to occur on December 24th, we have a great Christmas story.

I felt a cold breeze and huddled under my blanket. I inched my remote control out from under the blanket and flipped the channel. A furniture commercial. "The sale is this weekend only. No payment until next year." Let's see, isn't that just a little over a week from now?

My couch did have its signs of long use: the dog-clawed hole, the white stains, probably from my son's drool, the yellow streaks my daughter made with the marker that was supposed to be washable. Wanting a new couch, I had second thoughts about my commitment to a debt-free Christmas. Why had I agreed to that? Oh, yeah. Three credit cards we were still trying to get paid off, ghosts from Christmases past.

Enough of this. I aimed the remote, intending to turn off the television but hit channel four instead. *Die Hard*, another Christmas movie. The edited-for-network-television version where Bruce Willis jumps off the Nakatomi building after overdubbing to himself, "John, how the ... did you get into this ...?" Christmas with fireworks. Great. I considered the plot. A stranger comes to town—in this case a New York cop who is out of place in his marriage and cares nothing about life in Los Angeles. Even so, he risks his life to save a bunch of upper-middle-class Americans from the forces of evil, or rather from the people who want the money of the upper-middle-class Americans.

Christmas was starting to make sense. It wasn't about money or movies. But it was about caring. Didn't the Bible say Jesus was the light given to the world, and the darkness had trouble seeing it? If I let my light shine by caring for people, they would have the opportunity to see Jesus in me. And just maybe the day would come when Jesus could be born in their hearts.

With my head straight and my heart warmed, I turned off the television, stood up and stretched, and put my slippers back on. I headed for the bedroom, feeling refreshed, armed with a new determination that would get me through tomorrow's 20-percent-off sale.

Christmas Bonus
by Regina Golden

Lawrence Melton sank deep into his padded chair and closed his eyes to dream for a moment. The company was struggling, but he was the one who directed the software engineers. They needed him. He thanked God for a great job that let his family enjoy their ranch with the pool, putting green, and stable for the horses. Money was tight, but he was doing okay. The bank knew he was blessed, or they wouldn't have made the loan that let him keep his membership at the country club.

This would be the family's best Christmas ever, with expensive gifts piled under the tree to prove how much he cared. Shelly would open her first gift, see her diamond earrings and pendant, and throw her arms around him, saying, "I love you so much." Only God knew what she would do when she saw her diamond bracelet. Mark wasn't expecting a new car, not yet. He would be thrilled. With her new laptop and iPad, Hannah would be the envy of all her fifth-grade class-mates. All he was waiting for was his Christmas bonus.

At the sound of his office door closing, Larry opened his eyes and gave half a smile.

With the look of someone about to leave for a funeral, his boss took the seat in front of his desk. "We need to talk."

"I think I know the solution"—Larry put on his best look of confidence—"what to do about the project running behind schedule."

"That's not what I came to talk about. As of January 1, Dover Technology is closing its doors. We're all looking for jobs. You'll get a month's severance on your last paycheck, the end of this month. That's all there is." Looking about ready to cry, he stood and took a step toward the door. "I'm sorry. You're the first to know. I've got to make the announcement to everybody else."

Because of the icy roads and blowing snow, the drive home took longer than usual, which gave Larry more time to worry about how to break the news to Shelly. He made fresh tracks driving down the driveway into a winter wonderland that now looked dark, gray, and gloomy.

The first step past the door, he smelled ham and baked beans.

While dishing out the beans, Shelly looked up. "Hi, honey. How was your day?"

"Great." He gave her his customary kiss on the cheek while wondering what they would do without insurance the next time she had to see the doctor. He forced a smile. "Smells good."

Shelly gave him that I-know-you're-not-telling-me-something stare. "What's wrong? You look like your best friend just died."

"I guess I might as well tell you now." He pulled up the chair in the breakfast nook. "You better have a seat. Dover Technology is shutting down. I have three more weeks and a month's pay. No bonus. No more paychecks. What are we going to do? I can't pay the bills, let alone buy anything for Christmas."

Looking stunned, Shelly said nothing. At least she wasn't crying. Not yet.

"The job market isn't good," Larry said. "I'll do well to find something in six months. We'll have to sell the ranch, which could take even longer than finding a job. A month's pay can't stretch that far."

"You know, your dad always said having to trust God was a good thing." Shelly stood to get the plate of ham. "Maybe this can turn out to be a blessing."

"I don't know how."

"Neither do I, but we have to tell the kids. We should talk about it after supper."

When Larry prayed before the meal, his words felt empty, useless. He tried to laugh when Hannah told a joke she'd heard at school. He had to swallow hard when Mark talked about going to college at MIT and telling his senior-high friends that he was getting a Beemer for graduation. Thirty minutes at supper seemed like three hours.

Hannah pushed back from the table. "Can I be excused? I got homework."

Shelly shook her head. "In a minute. Daddy has an announcement to make first."

A half hour hadn't been enough for Larry to prepare what to say. A sip of iced tea. "I got laid off today."

"Neat," Hannah said. "Can I go—"

"No, Hannah," Mark said in a corrective tone. "That means Dad doesn't have a job. Not neat."

"It means there won't be much Christmas this year," Larry said. "I'm sorry, Mark, but there won't be a new BMW either. We'll put the ranch up for sale. I don't know…" He stopped to regain his composure, wiping the tears from his eyes. "I don't know how we're going to pay the light bill. It could be a long time before I find a job."

Hannah brightened. "If they turn off the lights, it would be like camping out."

"No it wouldn't," Mark said. "How would you charge your cell phone?" He looked at Mom, then Dad. "You have a lot of money in my college fund. We can use that."

"No, son. That's off-limits."

"I know you said a national disaster wouldn't be enough to touch those funds. But this is our family. Isn't that a much bigger emergency? As soon as I graduate, I can get a full-time job. It won't be much, but with what everybody else can do, we can make it."

Sally wrapped her hand into Larry's hand and smiled like it was Christmas morning. "This isn't your battle to fight alone, honey. We're in this together, and that's why, with God's help, everything will be all right."

Was that true? Too much had happened too fast. He rested his head in the palms of his hands and closed his eyes, trying to pull his thoughts together.

"Mom," Hannah said, "could I bake cookies to sell?"

"If we work together, I'm sure we can come up with all kinds of ideas."

"This morning I was devastated," Larry said, looking up with a smile. "I thought having no job and no bonus would ruin the holidays. Was I ever wrong. Having lots of stuff doesn't matter. Having everybody working together tells me Mom is exactly right. We won't have the ranch. So what? Mark may have to work his way through college, but we'll be okay. We have one another, and that's what matters. Knowing that is a priceless treasure.

You could call it a Christmas bonus."

Christmas Hope
by Ed Crumley

When Hitler was in power and our boys were fighting for freedom overseas, I was just a youngster at home, running from tree to tree, firing my imaginary rifle formed with my extended arms. "Ka-pow, ka-pow. Boom!" I had to make the battle sounds. I didn't even own a pop-gun. Whether fighting Indians in the west, Germans in Europe, or the British at Concord, I would be a better soldier if I had real equipment. At the top of my Christmas list I wrote: *a bugle, a drum,* and *a gun.*

These were the toys of my dreams because they made real sounds. With the bugle, I could gather my troops and save the settlers from the Indians. With the drum, I would lead my soldiers in a march. With a six-shooter that fired a red roll of gunpowder caps, I could ride with Roy Rogers, my singing cowboy hero, who put down the bad guys with his nickel-plated revolvers every Saturday afternoon on television.

The chance of getting my wishes was as likely as being drafted into the army at the age of seven. Steel and rubber were needed to manufacture tanks, jeeps, and rifles. Plastic was a newly invented novelty, not yet used for production of low-cost toys. The tin and cast-iron toys in the stores were beyond what most families could afford. Having a *wish* list meant it was okay to dream, but everybody knew those items wouldn't be under our tree on Christmas morning.

If army tanks had been made of wood, our forests would have been bare. Since they weren't, wood was affordable. Dad got out his tools and used his hands to make a memorable Christmas for me and my brother. The big boat rocked back and forth as if it were tossed by gigantic waves. The rocking horse came complete with mane, bridle, and saddle. The whoosh of the waves and the horse's whinny came whenever I chose to make the sounds. That wasn't all. Mom and Dad really splurged, because my brother and I both got cap pistols and pop-guns. With my bugle, I sounded the charge of the cavalry.

When our rich cousins showed up at the house on Christmas Day, they saw our presents and made jealous comments, exclaiming that we got more than they did. They thought that was unfair since their dad was an oilman and ours was a low-paid accountant. Part of their jealousy came from Granny living with us, so we got more attention and more gifts. She was quick to tell us how thankful we should be. "When I was a child out on the farm," she said, "I was happy to find an orange in my stocking."

As a teenager, I changed my wish list from toys to clothes. My brother and I begged for SMU football jerseys with 37 on the back, the number of our local hero, Doak Walker. A cool kid at school was the perfect image of Arthur Fonzarelli on the TV sitcom

Happy Days. I wanted the exact jacket and scarf the Fonz wore when he snapped his fingers and the girls came running. Funny, but on Christmas morning when I put them on, I didn't look like the Fonz. I knew I wouldn't be getting the girls I had imagined either.

What would make me happy? Would anything bring lasting satisfaction?

As an adult, I had received enough stuff to learn that enjoyment of a gift didn't depend on its cost. What I got, no matter how much it cost, wasn't all that important. Receiving a gift card was nice, but I found much more pleasure in giving.

When shopping, I looked for what others might enjoy. I lived for the excitement I saw on my boys' faces when they unwrapped G.I. Joe or their Hot Wheels. My heart warmed at the joyful tears in my wife's eyes when she lifted her blue-fox fur coat from its box.

When I became a grandparent, I reached what I thought was the peak of giving's great reward.

Emeline was an amazing miracle gift from God, having been conceived and brought into the world after many months of fervent prayer and a host of strenuous, highly expensive medical procedures. The crazy thing was, the more I thought I might be spoiling her, the more of a little servant's heart she displayed. She wasn't a half-pint Mother Teresa, thinking only about others— she liked her stuff. But she was constantly looking for ways to help people, giving from her own treasure chest. When her mother took her to sit on Santa's lap and recite her Christmas list, she insisted on giving him a present of one of her favorite toys. It wasn't a bribe. Since she had been given so much, she believed she should give too.

I thought I knew about giving, but she was teaching me.

We went to the American Girl Boutique & Bistro store because I had to see the latest fad in giving granddaughters everything they wanted. The entire store was dedicated to building relationships between girls and their dolls—pampering them both. Each doll had its own personal story, such as "Rebeckah," whose grandparents escaped the Holocaust, or "Molly," who grew up in colonial America. The store featured a complete beauty shop and *Bistro* for luncheon with her doll. While Molly was getting her hair done, Emeline and I browsed the store for new outfits—one for the doll and a matching dress for Emeline. This was a high-class place with prices to match.

As we left the store, our arms filled with boxes, I wondered how far we had come in sixty years. People were spending lots of money for something they believed was worthwhile, but I couldn't see how they could be having any more fun than what I had with my homemade rocking horse, my bugle, and my gun. Would the modern appetite for having more make people only want things for themselves and never learn the value of giving?

Emeline wanted more so she would have more to give, and that gave me Christmas hope.

Christmas Storage
by Joan Metzger

When I followed sis down the stairs into the musty smell of my basement, my grandson's question was still on my mind. *Will Santa bring toys to your house?* Two weeks before Christmas, still with no Christmas tree, no decorations, no lights on the house, how would Santa know to stop? By now I usually had my shopping done, but this year I hadn't even started. No matter how I felt, I couldn't disappoint my grandson.

One man's junk is another man's treasure, but what was all this stuff piled to the ceiling? Some had been Christmas presents, too good to throw away, yet not important enough to remain in use. "What's wrong with me, sis?" I rubbed my arms to take away the chill. "I have no Christmas spirit."

"I don't either." Susan paused. "Do you realize this will be our first Christmas without Mom? It won't be the same without her."

I squeezed past the Bowflex and stationary bike to reach the wooden storage racks. "Let's find the decorations. That's at least a start." My heart was heavier than the artificial tree I pulled from the shelf, the box thick with dust. "Mom always made Christmas a day to remember."

Susan pulled down a box and checked inside. "Yeah, it's the little things she did. Remember all the times we went to midnight mass, then met at her house for ham, eggs, and homemade cinnamon rolls?" Her tone was on the verge of tears. "We gotta cheer up. Mom wouldn't want us to be this sad."

In the corner sat what appeared to be a large chest, covered by a sheet. I sidestepped the it-was-just-what-I-always-wanted weight bench and yanked off the sheet. There it was: Mom's wooden camelback trunk, evidently left by movers when her house was cleared.

"Oh, my. Mom promised it would mine someday." I rubbed the lid like I was renewing my acquaintance with a long-lost friend. "One day I spent hours in her attic, looking at all the things she saved when I was a kid. My yearbooks. The blue ribbon I won in a jump-rope contest. I wonder what's in here now."

I grabbed the metal latch and pulled. The lid squeaked open and puffed its cedar aroma, which took me back to her attic. "Look at all this stuff." On top, a photo of Mom and Dad on Christmas Day, 1952. Tears spilled down my cheeks as I ran a finger across Dad's smiling face. He was so healthy back then. Why did a brain tumor have to take him away? He was still so young. Now Mom was gone too. I sank to the floor, unable to restrain my tears.

Bong... bong... bong...

I looked up the stairway, toward the sound of the grandfather clock in the hallway, beginning its chime.

"We need to get the decorations and go. I'll sift through the trunk later."

Wait. A small blue-velvet box lying beneath where the photo had been. I opened the box, slipped the ring on my finger, and held my hand up to the dim basement light. "Look, Susan. Mom's silver engagement ring." Fifty years later, the tiny diamond still sparkled like a twinkle-light on a Christmas tree.

What other treasures was the trunk hiding? I had to see. Sleet pelting against the basement window made me shiver. "Oh, this looks warm." I pulled out the afghan and wrapped it around my shoulders.

Susan joined me as I sat on the treadmill with a shoebox labeled "family pictures." I stopped at the picture of the whole clan, taken just before Dad died. Mom was smiling, but I saw fear in her eyes. My brothers and sisters had the same expression that I had, only halfway smiling, like we were posing at a funeral. Time to move on. I turned to the next picture: everyone trimming the Christmas tree. "Weren't we a happy lot?" I chuckled. "Here's one with you in Santa's lap."

For the first time since Mom died, I heard Susan laugh freely, like she was a kid about to open a present. Then I realized all this stuff hidden in storage was doing nobody any good. Memories shouldn't be concealed in a trunk. They should be brought out where people could enjoy them.

I looked at Susan. "Do you think these pictures and mementos would give our brothers and sisters a Christmas to remember, like when we were kids?"

"It's worth a try."

One by one, we sorted items into piles according to which one of us would most appreciate them. A baby quilt. Louis L'Amour paperbacks. Skeins of yarn. A notebook filled with poems.

"This is beginning to feel a lot like Christmas." I wanted the Betty Crocker cookbook for myself but handed it to Susan. "Here, you should have this."

"Why, because you don't think I can cook?" We laughed because we both knew better than that. This had been Mom's cooking book that we learned to follow like the Bible, which explained the aroma of spicy chili drifting down from the kitchen. Susan quickly grabbed the book and put it on her stack.

I stared at the 1952 Christmas photo. "Mom was three months pregnant with Nick when this picture was taken. He should have it." I looked back in the trunk. "What's this?" At first I thought it was a mouse. A yucky brown wallet with Nick's name engraved in gold, which didn't make sense. What was my brother's wallet doing here?

Behind the yellowed plastic windows were an odd-looking Iowa driver's license, a tattered Social Security card, and some *very* old family pictures. Tucked inside the bill compartment, a slip of rosebud-decorated writing paper: *To my dearest Nick on our tenth wedding anniversary.*

When I was younger, we always called my father "Dad"—or "Daddy." His name had been lost in forgotten memories until now. Amazed, I turned to Susan. "When Mom was pregnant, she said, 'Let's name the baby Nick. After Daddy.' This is Dad's wallet, not Nick's."

Like a daughter clinging to her daddy, I hugged the wallet. I wanted to shout, *Finder's keepers. It's mine*, but I knew it shouldn't be mine. I ran my fingers across the name. "Nick was born a month after Dad died. The wallet should go to him."

Surrounded by Mom's treasures, I anticipated the joy my brothers and sisters would have on Christmas morning. Santa would bring his toys for the kids, but Mom had given us memories that would last forever—memories that didn't belong in storage.

Christmas Magic
by Holly Smith

I wasn't sure there would be many presents under the Christmas tree, but that didn't keep me from dreaming. My three-year-old sister, Wendy, and I were counting the days. While waiting to go shopping with Mom, we stood next to our 1950 Oldsmobile and exchanged wishes.

Wendy didn't mind asking for the impossible. "I want a puppy," she said.

I shook my head. "That will never happen."

"Not a real dog," she said. "A stuffed one, so I can sleep with it."

While more realistic, I wasn't sure what we would get this year.

It was still dark when Wendy shook my shoulder and whispered, "It's Christmas!" We joined my brother in the hallway but had to wait until Mom and Dad said we could enter the living room. We were running before Dad finished saying, "Okay."

As soon as we rounded the corner, Wendy screamed, "It's a puppy!" She dropped to the floor to cuddle the little Dachshund, its leash wrapped around the doorknob. Its whole posterior wiggled with the happy flapping of its tail. It jumped onto Wendy's lap and gave her a syrupy lick. The tag tied with a red bow and ribbon around the puppy's neck said, *To Wendy... My name is Heidi.*

After cleaning up the wrapping paper, we readied the house for the relatives and neighbors whom Mom had invited for breakfast. Ornately decorated Christmas place-settings rested on poinsettia-embroidered white tablecloths, with gold and silver balls surrounding ceramic angels holding candles. Coffee steamed from Santa mugs, and the smell of hot chocolate made me thirsty. Name signs showed each guest where they were to sit. Mom decorated one card table especially for the children.

Everyone cheered when the scrambled egg casserole, sausage, cinnamon rolls, and biscuits and jam were set on the serving bar.

After breakfast, we rearranged the room so all the kids could be in the Nativity story. A hush fell over the audience when we entered wearing our costumes. I felt a reverent peace, like I was back in the first century, honoring the birth of the Savior. The glittered star hung by a thread above our cardboard stable. The shepherds wore long bathrobes and guided their cotton-dotted cardboard sheep with their wooden staffs. Cousin Tina was the shiny angel who pointed to the star.

Seated in her purple dress, Wendy cradled Betsy Wetsy in her arms, bundled in swaddling dish towels. My brother, as Joseph, stood behind Wendy and gazed adoringly down on the baby Jesus, his lips quivering uncharacteristically.

After the Bible passage was read, everyone sang the Christmas hymns: "Silent Night," "Away in the Manger," and "O Little Town of Bethlehem." Tears came to my eyes. God felt so close at that moment, like I was the reason for Jesus' birth two thousand years ago. My mind captured the picture with all its sounds and emotions, never to be forgotten. If I had been so deeply touched, I could only imagine how Mom's direction of the play—with all her hospitality and energy—had spoken to families who had never been exposed to the Christmas story.

Fifty years later, I pondered how I would spend the holidays with Mom and Wendy. We lived in different areas of the country, so we seldom had a chance for everyone to be together. I wanted this to be a special Christmas, especially for Wendy, because I knew about some of her financial struggles.

Wendy had the spark of energy and enthusiasm that set excitement ablaze in people's hearts. She made the perfect cheerleader in high school. Even as an adult, I loved the holidays because they were so thrilling to her. We always laughed and had fun together, but I worried that this year might be the sad exception. Her husband was barely surviving a dismal real estate market. Could she find joy in the season? How could I help her with the laughter she had so often given to me? We planned to see "The Nutcracker Suite" and tour an old home and estate, but I wanted more. I wished we could sing and perform skits like the old days.

I decided I could cheer up Wendy if I showered her with gifts. I didn't want a gentle rain. I wanted a downpour that was sure to make her feel special. She never objected to wearing secondhand clothes. As the

138

middle child, she accepted whatever hand-me-downs came her way. My job required designer clothes, so I had a wardrobe full of ways to shower Wendy with delight. Normally, the family exchanged practical gifts—even deciding to give *heart gifts* instead of anything elaborate. Not this year. Not for Wendy. From my closet, I gathered jackets, jewelry, leather handbags, blouses, sweaters and shipped them all to Mom's house in Austin.

On Christmas Eve, I picked up Wendy from the airport. The moment we walked into Mom's house, Wendy took one look at the Christmas tree and said, "Wow! Look at all the presents."

The next morning, as we passed out packages to the names written on the tags, Wendy's pile on the couch grew higher and higher. Overwhelmed with emotion, her eyes became teary. "It's just too much," she said. "I can't accept it." She had brought only the usual *heart gifts* for us.

Mom whispered to her, "Don't spoil your sister's joy of giving."

Wendy's face brightened like the morning she held her puppy for the first time. She tore through the paper and cried, ooh or aah in gratitude over each piece. She couldn't wait to try on the clothes and jewelry. After slipping back into the bedroom, she emerged to model each of the ensembles. Her whole countenance changed into a joyful euphoria. Her exaggerated modeling reminded me of our Sears Charm School days of pronounced stances, whirling and showing off, removing jackets, and hamming it up with humor. I snapped a picture of each outfit.

When Wendy perched on the couch in my pink

corduroy jacket, she giggled so hard she couldn't catch her breath. Her joy was contagious and we laughed uncontrollably. We sang carols, acted out our special song, and danced around the room.

Our day had all the magic of fifty years ago. I remembered how Wendy bubbled with joy when she held her puppy, how we performed the plays and sang songs together. In every way, the magic was about giving. That's what Mom had taught us for all those years.

There was greater joy in giving than receiving.

Christmas Truth
by Norma Vera

The West Texas holidays came with strong, cold winds and rolling tumbleweeds. If we were fortunate, it would snow once or twice during the winter. I loved everything about Christmas in spite of the windy weather.

My third-grade class and I waited with great anticipation as we helped our teacher decorate our classroom.

"What is Santa bringing you this year?" my friend asked.

I didn't want to answer. "I don't know," I said. "Something wonderful, I'm sure." I knew there would be no expensive toys. We always got school clothes and a few trinkets that Mom could barely afford after selling tamales. I never knew how poor we were until I started school and saw how the wealthy children dressed and celebrated Christmas.

When I came home, the smells of our freshly cut pine tree blended with other divine holiday aromas, including fresh-baked pies, making my mouth water.

The excitement grew as my sisters and I counted the remaining days until Christmas.

"Mom," I asked, my sisters chiming in, "don't forget we have to exchange gifts at school this Friday."

"I haven't forgotten." She gave us a quarter each. "Use it wisely!" she said, as we ran off to three neighborhood stores, seeking to find the best gifts our money could buy.

We scampered around, looking at everything the local stores had to offer. In those days, every store carried different toys. I bought a coloring book and small Santa-shaped candle. I had five cents left for an Orange Crush soda. As soon as we had paid for our gifts, we walked home, chitchatting with excitement, wondering who would draw our names and what kinds of gift we would receive. The rich children always gave the best gifts.

At the party, my teacher gave each child a Christmas storybook and a puzzle. The girl who drew my name gave me a coloring book and a box of sixteen crayons. I treasured both gifts.

School dismissed early, and on the bus ride home, I anticipated what Christmas would be like for us this year. In my Hispanic culture, we had more than the traditional ham, turkey, and dressing. There would be tamales, buñuelos, and other special treats. The lack of gifts didn't matter. All the love and laughter made Christmas my favorite day of the year.

On Christmas Eve, my sisters and I took part in the church's Christmas play. I was supposed to play the doll that sat under the Christmas tree, but one of the moms thought her daughter would make a prettier doll, so I had to play the part of a candy cane.

"That's okay, sis," my older sister said. "You'll make a great candy cane." I smiled and didn't complain, making the best of a painful situation.

That night I took some paper and wrote: *Dear God, will you please let it snow for Christmas?* I walked outside and let the wind blow the note out of my hand into the dark distant sky as if God might reach out, pick it up, and read it. In childish innocence, I prayed that God would get my note before dawn.

The next morning, I could hardly believe my eyes. A blanket of white covered our small town. While God was busy making snow during the night, Mom had been preparing our special treats, a small bag filled with candy, an orange, and an apple to put by our pillows as we slept. When my sisters and I opened our gifts, the toys were nothing to boast about—just a coloring book, some jacks, and a jump-rope. My valuable gifts were the two dresses I needed for school.

The snow quickly melted, and it was time to return to school. I wore the dress Mom had given me for Christmas.

"Did you have fun over the holidays?" my teacher asked the class. "Let's have everyone share about their Christmas."

My apprehension grew as one classmate after another stood and told about their wonderful gifts. Tommy, the smartest boy in class, got a Jr. Chemistry /Science Lab. Andy got a train set. Beverly, who sat in front of me, talked about her beautiful ballerina doll.

Each story made me feel the sting of my poverty. I rubbed my sweaty hands on my brand new dress as my turn drew near.

The children talked about all their wonderful

143

adventures—how they rode in a car or flew in a plane to their grandparents' homes in distant cities. One girl described Christmas shopping in New York. Some went snow skiing or ice skating.

I had stayed at home.

It was now my turn and I had no idea what to say? I didn't even get to be a pretend doll in the church play, much less get a doll for Christmas. I stammered and stuttered as I tried to put on an excited look. I described what I wished my Christmas had been like. I lied about the beautiful doll I didn't get and visiting the loving grandparents I didn't have." I looked at the teacher and wondered if she believed my fantasy.

I felt guilty, but at least I had survived the ordeal.

The teacher smiled—apparently convinced that everybody was proud of what they had received. "Friday," she said, "Everybody can bring one of your Christmas toys."

It was the worst day of my life.

How would I tell my friends that I didn't get anything special for Christmas? They would know I lied, and that was worse than not getting any toys.

Half a century later, the memories of that Christmas have probably been forgotten by everyone but me. I'll never forget it because it taught me a great lesson— to always be thankful for what we have. My mom did the best she could with the little we had, and her love carried us through those hard times.

Looking back, I realize that those precious memories were written in our hearts with the ink of my mother's love.

M.I.A. on Christmas Day
by Sally Sledge

All was in place for our traditional family celebration, but I had one remaining challenge. Since Mom's husband of fifty-nine years had passed away, how could I bring joy to her heart? Dad had always been there—loving and caring for Mom and making her laugh when times were tough. She missed him deeply and grieved for her own loss of mobility, her life confined to a wheelchair.

Determined to lift her spirits, I volunteered to take care of her on Christmas day.

The Christmas tree lights glistened, and packages overflowed beneath the branches—enough to excite even the oldest child. The aroma of wassail and pine needles filled the air and stirred pleasant memories. Garland with red velvet bows draped over the banister while mistletoe strategically hung in the entry to signal a merry season. Would this soothe the ache in Mom's heart?

For our Christmas dinner and gift-giving event, our families gathered at my sister and brother-in-law's home in Dallas. When their two sons were younger, they played a wise man and shepherd in the nativity play. Now grown and married, they towered over my small frame and displayed their strength by lifting me to the ceiling. They teased me like a little sister, and I provided enough comic relief that my brother-in-law nicknamed me "Silly." My oldest brother and his family joined us from San Antonio and my other brother contributed to the fun. Since we lived in different cities, we treasured this time of year when we could be together.

After we finished our feast and put the dishes away, we settled into the family room for our much-anticipated gift exchange. Playing Santa, the men select-ed packages from under the tree and delivered them to each person named on the gift tag. I sat at Mom's side and watched the mountain of presents grow beside her. Shiny packages with colorful ribbons displayed our love for her. Each gift held hopes of lifting her spirits and bringing her joy.

"Oh my, this is too much!" she said.

We knew this really meant *I'm overwhelmed with your expression of love.*

Due to the crippling effects of arthritis, Mom's fingers were crooked and stiff. At one time, those hands, now fragile and bent, were strong and took care of us. When I was a young girl, she taught me to sew and do needlepoint.

I placed a package on her lap and removed the ribbon to reveal one of her needlepoint projects, now made into a pillow.

"Oh, how beautiful!" she said.

She smiled and I knew she was pleased her work

had been memorialized. I savored the moment. She didn't feel sad or lonely because Dad wasn't there.

In a flurry, the other family members unwrapped their gifts and chattered wildly as the surprise inside was held up for all to see.

Since Mom's settled and everyone is focused on their gifts, this is the perfect time for me to slip away unnoticed to get my nephews' gifts out of the freezer. I'll be back before they notice I'm gone.

Now that the boys were older, they preferred the practical gift of steaks instead of gift cards or choices for younger boys. The four-car garage was located behind the house, two cars wide and two cars deep. The back half contained a vintage train set, boxes of family pictures, and other objects too precious to throw away. The freezer holding my steaks was in the far corner.

I went to the side door of the house and pushed the button to raise the garage door. I slipped outside, unnoticed, and walked to the freezer. I placed the first box of steaks in a gift bag.

The sound of a motor grinding broke the silence.

Startled, I looked up to see the light of day disappear as the garage door moved toward the ground. I gasped.

I can't move. Why don't my feet move?

I stared in disbelief as the metal door slammed against the cement. My heart pounded wildly. "Oh no," I whispered.

I'm trapped. No one knows I'm out here. I can't see anything. What if I run out of oxygen?

"H-e-l-p!" I yelled. My thoughts raced and I struggled to breathe.

No one can hear me and they won't even miss me until

Mom needs something or has to go to the bathroom. How do I get out of here? Oh God, help me.

I moved slowly toward the door, tripping over unknown obstacles.

Wasn't there a button to push or a handle to pull somewhere?

I found the garage door handle and pulled hard. It didn't budge.

Faint rays of light pierced the darkness and revealed shapes and shadows. My breathing slowed, and my thoughts became clearer.

There had to be a control button somewhere—but where?

I brushed my hand along the wall, feeling for a light switch, a button, or anything that could provide a way of escape. Then I felt it—a rectangular box on the wall with a button in the middle. I pushed hard, as if the button would not respond to a lighter touch. The motor came to life, moving the door upward. Light and fresh air poured in.

I'm saved! I can breathe!

I ducked under the half-raised door and ran to the house. Out of breath, I burst into the family room. "I was trapped in the garage!"

"What?" Apparently, they hadn't noticed I was gone. Silence fell over the room, and all eyes were on me.

"I went to the garage to get the steaks out of the freezer. The garage door closed behind me," I said.

"Oh, I closed it," my brother-in-law said. "I thought it was left open by mistake."

Mystery solved.

As I recounted the scene with great animation, my nephews and family doubled over with laughter.

Mom laughed so hard, she cried. Because of my plight, she received the perfect gift for Christmas—a heart full of joy and laughter.

"A cheerful heart is good medicine" (Proverbs 17:22 NLT).

Mirrored Holidays
by Sandy Wright

Christmas for six-year-olds was supposed to be magic, but for me they had become something to dread. When my Colorado mountains turned white with snow, dread seeped in. It was time for yet another kidney surgery. All I wanted was to see Santa, but instead we were headed to Texas for the holidays—to Grammy's home and then to see the doctors in white coats.

No sugar plums danced in my head. Instead, nightmares of hospitals and painful needles filled my dreams. Worse, because I had to fast, Grammy's home, which was filled with delicious smells of fresh baking, made me suffer all the more. But like a steady rhythm, two days before Christmas with my tummy growling, I took the predawn drive to the hospital.

Few Christmas lights twinkled along my path.

Instead the sweet smell of wassail and pine wreaths, the hospital smelled harshly of antiseptic cleaners. There were no red or green lights. The bright fluorescents colored everything white on white. This was no place for carolers.

The doctors swarmed around me like bumblebees ready to sting. When the nurse came to draw blood, I hid under the giant bed. She tried to ease my fright by wrapping my throbbing finger to look like bunny ears, but nothing could stop my body from trembling. The pattern was set. I knew what was coming next, the operating room.

"Mommy—Daddy, don't let him take me."

My doctor smiled like a loving dad and scooped me up in his arms. I strained to grab for my mom and dad but he held me tight. By the time we entered the elevator, I quit fighting, too frightened to say another word.

Gently, he placed me on the operating table and turned to wash up. The room was a buzz of activity as the nurses and attendants readied for surgery. No one was looking at me. Quietly, I slipped off the table and in a flash was out the door, my hospital gown flapping. Pounding footsteps came from behind me, and two wide arms corralled me in the corner.

"Just where do you think you're going?" the doctor asked.

My cough got his attention. He put his stethoscope to my chest and sighed. "She's got a cold. We have to postpone."

His words made my eyes pop wide open. Like a Cheshire cat, I grinned. I had been spared.

We zipped back to my Grammy's home where I ate a huge slice of pumpkin pie. With my sister and cousins, I walked on stilts and played tag. When my uncle grabbed me by the ankles and lifted me up, I saw what a lighted Christmas tree looked like upside down. This was everything I imagined Christmas should be.

The phone rang, and the magic disappeared.

An emergency at the oil rig required my dad, a geological engineer, to return to the Colorado Rockies to work. Bent over the trunk of the car, my mom wiggled my Grammy's ham among our suitcases, and I said goodbye to Christmas. I didn't cry—I was used to losing Christmas.

The sun turned orange before it dropped below the horizon and the sky darkened. Hours passed, and I drifted in and out of sleep. When the car began a steep climb up a mountain pass, I woke and pressed my nose against the cold window. The sky was a mass of twinkling stars. Filled with awe, I giggled because I was sure God had sprinkled Christmas lights across the sky.

The towering oil rig dotted the horizon with dazzling lights. It was the biggest Christmas tree I had ever seen. I grinned. Santa would know how to find me.

Daddy slowed to maneuver the rugged rig road, but the tires dropped into one pot hole after another. My sister, Lana, and I bounced like balls. It was so different than the ride I had taken to the hospital. This one felt like a rollercoaster ride, and we squealed with delight

It seemed that the motors churned and steel pipes clanked with a steady cadence of "Jingle Bells." My metallic Christmas tree-rig towered high above my head. Its mass of crisscrossed steel was bright with lights, making Christmas Eve night almost as light as the day. I arched my neck to see the "crow's nest" at the very top.

Daddy plopped an oversized hardhat onto my head. He laughed as it wobbled there. "You look like a bobble-head doll." He took my hand and showed me and my sister his world of grease, giant clamps, and gauges.

It was now my world too.

While my dad shouted to a man in a yellow hard hat, I watched men slip and slide across the oil-slick floor. They moved like dancers who had practiced every step and turn. The floor's steady vibration pulsed through my legs. The rhythm of the rig became my rhythm, and I wanted to dance and glide with the roughnecks.

Scruffy men stopped throwing the chain around the pipe and gathered around my sister and me. Their approach reminded me of the doctors and nurses who loomed over me. I stumbled back, wanting my father to save me, but he didn't turn around.

A squatty man with an oil-smeared, toothless grin held out his hand.

I gasped. His thumb was missing.

He motioned to the rigging, making it clear that I needed to be careful. We'd never been this close to rough-necks, and they'd never seen children on the rig before. Christmas Eve allowed such things.

Later, while my dad worked, off-duty men repeatedly drug sleds up the snow-covered hill—just for us. They held us tight and in a mad dash we jumped onto the sled and careened down the slippery slope. My fears of strangers vanished like melting snowflakes. These were not the white-coated hospital staff. They were my grubby friends in greasy overalls.

Over the open fire pit, my mom layered ham, jellied cranberry, and green beans onto tin foil and made individual packets. Was it the open air, or having fun friends around, or maybe just not having to spend

Christmas Eve in a hospital? Whatever it was, this was the best Christmas Eve dinner I ever ate.

At dusk, my dad pointed to the rig. High on the crow's nest, a plump man in red long-handles grabbed the zip line and let his body fly to the ground. He looked like Santa. The rig had all the magic of Christmas.

That night, Lana and I lay at opposite ends of the small trailer's bed. Unlike the sterile hospital bed where I shook in fear, on this bed, I felt cozy and relaxed, the sensations of the pounding rig creating the rhythm of "O Holy Night." As I let my fingers slide over the smooth hard-hat, I sniffed the pungent smells inside my dad's work trailer. Unlike the hospital smells, they didn't frighten me.

Hospitals and oil fields were both unfamiliar worlds. Neither was enticing. Yet in a pulsating cadence, my time in the oil field had miraculously eased my dread of the holidays.

Christmas was fun.

Christmas Crisis
by Larry Hurlbut

December 21, 2004, 7:00 a.m. I felt the pressure as I stepped onto the rapid-transit bus. Only three days were left to complete what should be three weeks of work, all because two people in my department had quit, leaving me to manage the project short-handed. I would have to do much of the work myself, preparing the documents for the renovation of a thirty-five story office building listed on the National Historic Register.

At the back of the bus, I peered out the fogged window and watched the cars moving slowly, bumper to bumper, in the rush-hour traffic. Nobody was getting anywhere fast, the perfect picture of my team's progress. How was I going to get everything done? I wanted to take time off and spend Christmas with my children, to celebrate and be filled with the peace and joy announced by the angels at the time of Christ's birth. I could see no way that was going to happen. I closed my eyes, trying to rest.

Off the bus, I quickly walked the half-block to the office. After a glance around the room to be sure everybody was working, I discussed with Matt, a young team member, what needed to be done. I emphasized the importance of each person's task. I'd had many challenging assignments in my career, but I knew this was more than I could do. The same was true for everybody else. It seemed, for one reason or another, we were always under pressure.

An hour later, I felt a slight discomfort in my chest. Heartburn again. I reached into the compartment of my shoulder bag for my pills. Nothing. Then I remembered. I had left the bottle at home, sitting on the bathroom counter.

Okay, back to work. Living through discomfort was a normal part of my routine. I'd just have to take my heartburn medicine when I got home. Then I could relax for the evening.

I was halfway down the fourth page of the room-finish schedule when I felt like somebody had hit me in the chest. Intense pain. Was I having a heart attack? Surely not. But I couldn't help wondering if I was about to die. No, it couldn't be that. I needed my heartburn medicine.

"Matt, I'm not feeling well." I peered into the first cubicle. "Would you drive me to the Park-and-Ride so I can take my medication? I don't think I can make it through the rest of the day."

When I buckled my seatbelt, the pain hadn't subsided. "Take the expressway," I said weakly. "It's not the most direct route, but it takes us near the hospital where my doctor's office is located. If I'm not better by the time we reach the hospital exit, you need to take me there."

I relaxed enough to catch a half-decent breath and

156

felt a little relief. Just heartburn, like all the other times when I had gone to the emergency room. Each time, after they ran all their tests, the diagnosis was the same. The pain wasn't heart-related.

"You don't need to exit," I said. "Go on to the Park-and-Ride."

Six exits later, the pain increased significantly—worse than anything I had previously experienced. Bad enough to think I might not take another breath. "Matt, you better turn around. I think I'm having a heart attack." Quickly, I spouted directions to the emergency room, thinking I might lose consciousness, praying that I would reach the doctors before I passed out.

The hospital doors were like an oasis seen by a man crossing the desert without water. "Thank you, Lord," I said, gathering my strength. I stumbled past the automatic doors to face the receptionist. "I have this terrible pain in my chest. I think I'm having a heart attack."

In seconds, I was riding a gurney down the corridor toward the elevator, with an IV in my arm.

"What's the pain?" one nurse asked in a rushed, desperate tone.

"One to ten, what's the pain," the other nurse shouted. "Talk to me!"

They kept asking, but I wasn't answering. I seemed to be drifting away. A faint, male voice said, "You are having a heart attack."

I opened my eyes to white walls and bright lights. This didn't look like Heaven. I was lying in a hospital bed surrounded by monitors that registered my vital signs. Evidently, I was still alive, but for how long? The strange beeping of the medical equipment made me wonder. When the nurse came in, I had to know. "What happened to me?" I asked.

"The doctor put a stent in one of your main arteries. There was no other blockage." She smiled and patted my hand. "Your vital signs are normal. If you continue to improve, you'll be discharged in a day or two."

I joyfully expressed my gratitude. "Praise God," I said. "Thank you. Thank you. Thank you, Lord! You saved my life today."

My mind was suddenly filled with memories of another time of crisis in Los Angeles, thirty years ago when I surrendered my heart to Jesus and walked from my dark world into his marvelous light. I wasn't looking for him, but he was looking for me, filling me with the Holy Spirit.

I became his child.

Two days before Christmas, my son, John, came to drive me home. The sun was dropping beneath the horizon, leaving the Christmas lights to brighten the darkness and remind everyone of God's gift of life. I didn't need a reminder. Life on Earth is but a vapor, appearing for a little while, then suddenly gone. My Lord had walked with me through the valley of the shadow of death. I had no reason to fear. Whenever my home in Heaven is finished, I would be ready to go.

Because of Christ, wherever I was, whether at work or with my family, I could relax and avoid the pressure. My only crisis was my need to say more than "Merry Christmas." I needed to express to others the depth of God's love.

Holiday Feeling
by Mary Sefzik

As I was being driven to Grandma's house, knowing where I was going and the familiar roar of the tires on different pavements brought back memories of Christmases when I was a kid. Two of my grandparents were already in Heaven, and my two remaining grandparents were another year older. Would the smells be familiar when Grandma opened the door? I wondered if she would take me on a tour like before. I looked forward to being led around the living room, to refresh joyful memories, and hear something new.

After five long hours in the car, Grandma's steaming bowl of hamburger soup tasted extra good. "Grandma," I said, "my soup never tastes as good as yours. What do you put in it?"

"Something different every time. I put noodles and potatoes in this batch. Have you tried the new pretzel crackers?" She put the crackers at my fingertips. "They were on sale at Wal-Mart last week. Buy one, get one free."

I bit into one. Crunchy, with more thickness than a

potato chip. And tasty, with plenty of salt. "You'd make a great mystery shopper."

"You never know what they'll come out with next. I'll try anything once." Her footsteps moved toward the table of goodies. "What do you want for dessert? I've got coconut and chocolate pie, strawberry pound cake, and M & M cookies. There's also a pumpkin roll and a big box of chocolates."

So many choices, but I knew what I liked best. "Oh, I'll have the pumpkin roll," I said with delight. I savored my last spoonful of soup, then bit into the slice of pumpkin roll, moist and sweet.

"Have you seen my beanie baby tree?" Grandma asked.

"No." I knew how popular beanie babies were, but a tree full of them was something new.

When Grandma took my hand, I knew the annual Christmas tour was about to begin. She put my hand on something small and fuzzy. "Check out the nose on that elf. Isn't he something?"

"Yes, it feels round and hard, like a tiny jawbreaker."

She led me a few steps across the room. "Take a good look at this Santa Claus. What is he holding?"

The shape of cubes. Soft bows. "They're Christmas presents." I wondered what presents I would get to open in the morning.

The sound of music. Someone singing. Grandma pulled me closer so I could feel what she was showing me. "What do you think of my singing soldier?"

I felt his arms and legs, straight like he was standing at attention. "He's beautiful. And he has a great voice."

Through the doorway, I smelled the deodorant soap, felt the lavatory, and knew I was in the bathroom.

"Look," Grandma said. "This year I even put up a tree in here." She was the best tour guide because nothing was off limits to my fingers. She was always handing me something and saying, "Tell me what this is" or "I bet you haven't seen one of these before."

At the dining room table, I felt the Christmas tree standing in the center. When I touched the tiny cloth soldier hanging from the limb, I heard two other soldiers fly off the tree and hit the table. "Sorry." I picked them up and tried to put them back in place but couldn't make them stay.

"Don't worry about it. I'll put them back later. What good are Christmas decorations if you can't touch them? Here, hold this."

I immediately recognized the soft fur and the sound of his voice. The singing Santa bear, who was almost as tall as I was. As I gave him a hug and smiled, I heard the click. Grandma had taken my picture.

I took my time enjoying every surprise—stuffed elves perched in chairs, a glass nativity scene on the coffee table, and bulging stockings for everyone, even the dog.

"Do you remember this?" Grandma asked, with a rustling that made me think she had pulled something from a paper sack.

I felt the crumpled dress, the face, and the wings. "Wow! I made this angel in the fifth grade. I can't believe you still have it."

"Every year, it takes its place of honor in the center of the table that's covered with Christmas cards."

My hands were drawn to the pile of presents in the

161

living room. I resisted the urge to shake them, or ask which ones had my name on them.

"Good night, sweet girl." Grandpa said.

It was time for bed. I hugged him, remembering how many times on Christmas Eve he had kissed me on the cheek and whispered, "Granddad loves you"— my last memory before I drifted off to sleep.

Grandma followed me into the bedroom and pulled down the covers. "I saw Santa Claus yesterday," she said. "He told me to tell you Santa loves you and he'll never forget you."

I hadn't sat on Santa's lap for years, but it was comforting to know I was still on his Nice list. I thought of the jovial Santa at the mall, who always made me smile. His hearty "Ho-ho-ho. It's good to see you. Come and sit on Santa's lap" was a sound that still rang in my ear. He encouraged me to touch his long, white beard, his belt, and his big boots. I got to ring his sleigh bells. He handed me a candy cane and asked, "Now what do you want for Christmas this year?" I rattled off a list of dolls, games, and toys while Dad captured the moment with his camera.

Now, Grandma had helped me see those moments again.

"Oh," Grandma said, "I forgot to show you this— another Santa Claus. He tells the story of *The Night Before Christmas*. I got him at the hospital for ten dollars, the last one they had."

Grandma and her Christmas bargains. I snuggled beneath the soft sheets and prepared to enjoy a tradition lost since childhood—a bedtime story. "Twas the night before Christmas and all through the house, not a creature was stirring not even a mouse..." As I listened to the Christmas poem, my mind went back to that pile of presents. What fun game had Grandma found this year? How many folded-up one-dollar bills would I find in my stocking? I strained to hear the faint jingle of Santa's sleigh bells. I felt like a child again, basking in the awe and wonder of Christmas.

I was abundantly blessed. Grandma loved me. Granddad loved me. Santa loved me. And because God loved us all, we could have peace and joy in the world.

Counting the Days
by Renee Alford Sessions

From the time the doctor set December 7 as the due date, Nora dreamed of having her baby on Christmas day. She thought it would be wonderful, although a most unlikely possibility, if she could celebrate her baby's birthday on the same day the family gathered to remember the birth of Jesus.

Nora and her husband, Bill, talked about how the December birth would affect their plans for the holidays. Shopping would have to be finished early. There was putting up decorations and baking and Christmas parties to attend. Would she be able to do those things? She needed a plan—a plan for unknown variables.

Nora worked at warp speed. She felt frantic at times, but settled into her role as fulltime homemaker, caring for her toddler, John. When she decorated the nursery, Bill offered to hang the mirror and curtains. "No," she said, "that's fine. I have everything under control." Actually, *control* was what she wanted so badly to maintain, but as she counted the days, she felt like she had less and less control.

Summer days of toddler swim lessons and morning strolls gave way to autumn afternoons with shorter walks and more rest. She inventoried baby clothes, diapers, and bedding items, and placed everything neatly in drawers and on shelves. It was time to face the holidays.

The day before Thanksgiving, she finished baking and had her Christmas shopping list ready. Nothing could be left to chance. She wanted no last-minute surprises other than the one she couldn't control.

On the Friday after Thanksgiving, she and Bill were folding laundry while John played in his room.

"Do you still want to go to the park today?" Bill asked. "We can take the soccer ball for John."

"That'd be great, but I need to organize the pantry first. Then we can go."

"Didn't you do that last week? You're redoing what you've already done, aren't you?"

She shrugged. "I don't know. Did I? Oh, yes, I guess I did. We can go."

On December 7, Nora waddled into Dr. Garza's office and plopped onto the padded chair in the waiting room.

"Mrs. Estes, are you ready to see the doctor?" Angie asked from behind the counter.

"Don't I look like I'm ready?"

Angie joined Nora's laughter. "Today's the big day, isn't it? Do you think this little one wants a few more days of warm weather or does he want to see his shadow?"

"Don't ask me. I'm just the producer of this show."

Nora followed the nurse down the hall to the

examination room. She knew the drill. The ultrasound would confirm the baby's position. She covered her swollen abdomen with a warm blanket, gently rubbed the tightly-stretched skin, and spoke to the child she longed to see. "Little one, it won't be long now." Tears filled her eyes. *Get control of yourself.*

Worn and weary, she needed to hear her precious baby's heartbeat. She had come for that alone.

Dr. Garza walked in. "Congratulations, Mom, you're almost to the finish line." He was ten years her senior, with a salt-and-pepper mustache that gave a mischievous flavor to an otherwise serious occupation. "How are you feeling?"

"Fine." All things considered, she didn't think she was lying. "Are you sure I'm not carrying two in here?" She inhaled, then exhaled slowly, like the burden was too great to bear.

Dr. Garza laughed as he reached for his stethoscope. "Remember, I told you to expect the weight gain during the last trimester. The baby looks healthy. Let's listen to her heart."

Nora braced for the cold instrument to glide over her belly. The heartbeat pounded clearly. Tears again. She swallowed hard. "Thanks. I needed to hear that sound today."

"Let's talk about the next few days and hope that it doesn't turn into weeks. I want to see you every day. If you feel contractions, you know what to do. The second time around, you never know, so let's keep a careful watch on this Christmas baby." His eyes twinkled.

"Oh, that would be wonderful. Could the wait possibly be that long?"

"Possibly, but not likely."

"If the baby hasn't come by Christmas Eve, could we induce labor on Christmas day?"

"By then, we might want to do that, but another doctor will have to handle the delivery. I'll be out of town."

At seven days past due, Nora was sitting cross-legged on the living room floor, wrapping a few presents, worried that the baby's coming would interrupt something important. She didn't want to give birth at Bill's company Christmas party or at church on Christmas Eve. She especially didn't care to speculate on Christmas day, not with the doctor out of town.

By the end of the following week, Nora responded in sound bites to eager friends who knew the baby was past-due: "Baby's healthy. Mom's healthy. We're just waiting on Santa." Others were excited. Nora was just tired of waiting. She cooked and played with John to ease her anxiety.

On Saturday night, Nora glanced at the calendar and shook her head. By now the baby should be three weeks old and into a routine. "There's a reason," she whispered. *I'm not in control here. I can't do this without you, Lord. Please be with me.*

Christmas week came with snow, cold and damp. Nora huddled with John on the rug in front of the fireplace, building a lop-sided log cabin, working beneath the lights of the Christmas tree beside them.

John said, "See that?"

"See what, babe?"

"Your shirt. Look! It's moving."

Nora laughed as she pulled John's hand onto the top of her stomach. "Feel. Your baby brother is moving." Through a make-believe microphone, she imitated John's voice: "This is your brother speaking. Come out with your hands up."

On Christmas Eve, Nora's parents arrived in anticipation of more than just presents under the tree.

"Wow!" Nora's father looked at how big she was and gave her a hug. "It's time to get this show on the road, girl."

"Well, I've finally figured out, it's not my show."

On New Year's Day in the comfort of her home, Nora wrote in her journal: *The hardest part was encouraging others not to change their routine. I wanted to keep our Christmas tradition with all its warmth and laughter. We hung popcorn garlands on the tree. We made gingerbread cookies for the neighbors. On Christmas Eve we went caroling to encourage peace on earth and goodwill toward men. Then on Christmas day, family and friends gathered around my hospital bed to sing, 'Away in the Manger,' as I held my newborn son.*

That Christmas of 1983, Nora finished counting the days and held the sweetest gift ever.

Headless Wise Men
by Richie Wines

Ready or not, it was the day after Thanksgiving—Christmas decoration time. Surely the pilgrims had more than twelve hours to digest their turkey dinner before having to put up Christmas lights. My wife already had Johnny Mathis Christmas carols playing on the stereo, so there was no way I could enjoy watching a football game on television. I groaned as I climbed the creaking steps into the attic, wanting this year's decorating to go smoothly and quickly.

The number of boxes filled with Christmas stuff was more than I remembered putting there. Each time I handed one down to my wife, another seemed to take its place. I broke into a sweat and pulled two muscles in my back before I got to the final box, which looked like a duct-taped suitcase that had been abandoned at the airport luggage carousel. I climbed down to see the living room, which looked like the cluttered warehouse scene of *Raiders of the Lost Ark*. Without help, this was going to be a long day.

My kids tore into the boxes. Five-year-old Emily

unwrapped the nativity scene while three-year-old Mitchell set the pieces around his plastic dinosaur. We soon had a clipped-wing angel, an armless Joseph, and two headless wise men. With help like this, I might not finish in a week.

I used superglue to repair Joseph and the wise men. Oh, no. As I arranged the nativity scene on the end table, I recognized a problem with one of the wise men. His head was turned backward. I positioned the ill-fated figure behind the cow, hoping nobody would notice.

We unpacked Christmas bears, stockings, and cookie jars. The tarnished brass merry-go-round was supposed to be powered by candles, but the hot summer had transformed the candles into amoeba-like blobs. The Styrofoam Frosty Snowman underneath was covered in wax that cemented him to a cartoon penguin. The new creation had the weirdness of a Salvador Dali sculpture. I couldn't decide whether I should throw it away or sell it as art to the highest Ebay bidder.

Our artificial Christmas tree was big enough to have its own ecosystem, and probably would have if it didn't have to be disassembled and stored in its box. Squirrels could live there, along with barn owls, monkeys, and a few Keebler elves. Out of the enormous box, I pulled a thousand branches, each marked on its wire base with a tiny color-coded sticker with letters from AAA to ZZZ, indicating where each limb attached to the trunk. Unfortunately, half the stickers had fallen off. By the time I finished guessing and sticking branches into holes, the tree looked like a shrub trimmed by a drunken Edward Scissorhands.

The tree took nine strands of lights and enough

170

garland to have decked the halls of the Empire State Building. When I plugged in the lights, they flashed and went black. Then I remembered. I could only chain four strands into a single string. Any more would blow a fuse. After spending thirty minutes searching forty-three boxes, I couldn't find a replacement fuse.

"I need to go to Lowe's," I said, thankful to get away from the mess.

"Take the kids with you," my wife said.

With the kids' help, I took an extra hour to find a replacement pack of 100 fuses.

I swapped the fuses and plugged in the lights. Three strands had every other light working with a steady beam while three others blinked on and off. Since I had a college degree, I was sure I could figure this out. Eighteen swapped lights and an hour later, I had four strands that half-worked, four that blinked, and one that worked as long as I pushed down on the third light from the plug. Sometimes experience is the best teacher. I knew exactly what to do. After another trip to buy lights at Lowe's, I had the whole tree lit up.

The tree was huge so it could hold all our ornaments. Six boxes contained yearly ornaments dating back to 1972, art ornaments in various states of disrepair, and the cartoon ornaments. Then there were figurine ornaments, glass ornaments, and crocheted ornaments. We couldn't leave out the paper ornaments, metal ornaments, and clay ornaments.

Was there anything that couldn't be used to make a Santa ornament? Apparently not. We had Santa ornaments made from Coke cans, light bulbs, and pipe cleaners. Others were made from beans, clothespins, and dried okra. Then there were the ones made from spent shotgun shells, dominoes, and gourds.

Emily was born in 2003, and Mitchell came two years later. I found sixteen "Baby's First Christmas" ornaments for Emily. Where were Mitchell's ornaments? Not a single one was dated 2005.

We had a dozen ornaments that either talked or sang. They said phrases like "Ho-ho-ho," "Merry Christmas," or "Grandma loves you." Or they sang "Rudolph the Red-Nosed Reindeer" or the Oklahoma University fight song. I expected them to be out-of-tune, but what I heard was worse. They sounded like a heavy-breathing Darth Vader with a bad cold. Any movement set them off. I brushed a branch and thought I heard an ornament say, "Luke, I am your father," set to a funeral dirge bagpipe chorus of "Jingle Bells."

My kids hung ornaments, all in a row along the bottom of the tree, at their eye level. I tried to be sure they only had the unbreakable ones, but the ceramic drummer boy and crystal angel slipped by. "Be careful with that," I said, trying not to shout.

Our ninety-five-pound Labrador, Jake, rushed in from outside, wagging his tail like a club. My kids' eye level was directly in his strike zone. His tail struck a shiny ball ornament, sending it over the couch where it shattered on the bricks above the fireplace, which would be a home run in any American League Doggie Ballpark.

Somewhere between the crocheted reindeer and the gingerbread angels, I slowed down long enough to notice the wonder on my kid's faces. They were soaking up the holiday atmosphere like they thought it was Christmas Eve, dancing and singing and laughing. If I had paid attention earlier, the day would have been much more fun.

As the smell of apple cider and the sound of Johnny Mathis Christmas carols filled the house, I was thrilled to see my kids so happy. My tiredness melted away. Christmas was more than decorations, parties, and gifts. The love of family, the expectations of youth, and the wonder of how God became man—these were the things that truly made this the most wonderful time of the year.

I joined my kids and Johnny in a chorus of "Deck the Halls" while I looked for an open bough to hang a tongue depressor Santa.

A Push and a Shove
by Carolyn K. Knefely

The Christmas tree was cut. All eight-year-old Lindy needed to do was set it up in the living room, but how? Mom refused to help, but said Lindy and her stepbrothers and stepsister could figure out a way. A box filled with sand should work.

The four of them crossed the street to the playground and filled their carton with sand, but it was too heavy for any one of them to carry. By herself, Lindy couldn't even push it across the grass to the road. "Come on, let's all push," she said.

"I'm cold," Susie, her six-year-old stepsister, said. "You're mean, and I don't have to do what you say. My mommy said so." She didn't want to be part of the team, which was nothing new, but with further encouragement, she relented.

With a push and a shove, a tug and a pull, the battered cardboard box inched closer to the asphalt road. "We can make it," Lindy said. "Everybody push at the same time." With another push and a shove, a tug and a pull, the box moved onto the icy road.

Lindy gave the box another shove, but it moved only an inch. Jason, Lindy's youngest brother grabbed the side of the box and yelled, "Everybody, now!" Like a duck sliding across a frozen pond, the box slid almost six feet.

Jason was now enjoying this game. His blonde hair curled out from under his leather football helmet. In true football style, he tackled the job without complaint and with all-out effort. He didn't know why the box had to go from the playground to the living room, but he obviously liked being part of the fun.

By the time they reached the house, the sides of the carton looked more round than square. How could they get it up the steps? "Everybody has to lift at the same time," Lindy said.

With a unified heave and ho, the four frozen children lifted their treasure and dropped it with a thud onto the empty corner of the living room. While they lay on the floor, thawing out, Mom recited what was left to be done.

The boys raced to the back yard to get the freshly cut tree. The girls carried their coats to their room and returned with their arms laden with homemade ornaments.

Lindy inhaled the sweet cedar smell and forgot all about being cold. She sighed when the boys planted the tree in the sand. It wouldn't stay up.

"We gotta get a bigger box and more sand," Jason said.

"I can hold it up," the youngest said.

Lindy stomped off, defeated. "Well, trees don't belong inside a house anyway. Why do we need a darn ole Christmas tree?"

Mom smiled, apparently pleased with the children's effort. "All we need is a nail, some string, and a prayer." Standing on a bar stool, Mom hammered a nail into the ceiling and tied a piece of twine from the nail to the top of the tree.

The children stepped back to admire their work. It was a triumph to behold. They strung construction paper chains of red and green in a spiral from the top to the bottom. Strings of popcorn and cranberries were scalloped in lacy loops with pointed peaks and rounded valleys. They added snowflake cutouts, candy canes, and aluminum-foil ice sickles. God's sunlight added the sparkle.

"We did it."

"It's beautiful."

"Humph."

"Touchdown!"

"I am proud of all of you," Mom said.

The children looked at the tree, then at one another with smiling faces and shining spirits. They had never seen anything so beautiful. They had never felt more satisfied.

With a push and a shove, a tug and a pull, a box filled with sand, a nail and a piece of twine, a new family was joined and a prayer was answered.

A Christmas tree in the corner of the living room bound them together with the true gift of Christmas—love.

Seeing Is Believing
by Ronda DeBeaux

Adults don't believe in Santa Claus, do they? Believing is for kids, not grown-ups. I was a grandmother and a Christian, which should have been sufficient reason to hold rigidly to biblical truth and reject all fairy tales. Not me. Maybe I never really grew up, because I still wanted to believe. "Oh, Santa's real," I said, smiling, but with a serious tone that left people wondering. Some laughed. Others looked at me like they thought I might be crazy.

As a child, I couldn't wait for Santa to come. I asked the typical questions: "Mommy, we don't have a chimney, so how will he bring the presents in? Do reindeer really fly? How can he deliver presents to the whole world in one night?" I wasn't really looking for an answer. I just wanted enough support to be sure my believing hadn't been wasted. On Christmas Eve, I left milk and homemade chocolate-chip cookies. The next morning, the empty glass and plate were proof that Santa had come.

On a clear Texas night, chilly but never with snow,

I scanned the sky, searching for the brightest star. I asked, "Which one is the Star of Bethlehem?—the one the wise men followed." I didn't have to find the star to believe the story was true. Since Christmas was about giving, about peace and goodwill toward men, Santa and Jesus would make good friends.

When I taught my children the Christian and Santa traditions, the magic of Christmas became even more real. Still, conflict swirled in my mind. Why did I need to believe in Santa? A year after my children no longer believed, I went on a mission trip to Finland.

The Finnish believe in Santa Claus, although they call him Joulupukki. They consider Finland his homeland. According to legend, a hundred years ago a lost traveler saw him near a mysterious and secluded mountain called Korvatunturi in Lapland, near the Russian border. He visited the children near the Arctic Circle and eventually founded a village near the small town of Rovaniemi. The people named it Santa Claus Village, and he visited every day.

In late November, I arrived with the mission team in Helsinki and spent several days teaching at the Bible college. Our host family welcomed us warmly, taught us many of their customs, and treated us to their traditional dishes. One evening they held an early Christmas celebration for us.

Snow fell almost every day in this dreamlike world. We took long walks among great snowy fir trees, battled with snowballs, and made snow angels. On our last night, we went sledding. For a girl who had grown up in Texas, this was a magical time.

On the ten-hour train to the Finnish Lapland on the next day, I stared in wide-eyed wonder at the countryside. Forests of pine and fir trees stretched for miles. Clothed in snowy cloaks, the trees sparkled like diamonds. Tears gathered in my eyes. The beauty took my breath away as I lived my dream. We arrived in the Arctic village of Rovaniemi late in the evening.

A lovely Finnish woman, with bright blue eyes set in a round, rosy-cheeked face, met our train. In her accented voice she asked with a smile, "Are you Texas?"

Laughing, we replied, "Yes, we are from Texas."

Our hostess served a dinner of shepherd's pie made from reindeer meat.

The next day we walked through the village square. A fresh dusting of snow covered the town. We wandered through shops filled with various native crafts and tourist trinkets. The wintry sights and jingle-bell sounds of Christmas and Santa Claus were everywhere. I was lost in a Christmas world, filled with peace and goodwill.

When our hostess said we would visit Santa Claus Village, I remained calm on the outside, but I was leaping for joy on the inside. The eight-mile drive took forever. Eventually the tall spire of the main building came into view.

I strolled through the village with childlike wonder. Snow blanketed everything. Quaint brick paths wandered between cozy log buildings. The snow was cleanly swept off the sidewalks and piled in mounds alongside. Reindeer were resting in their pen. After touring the post office where children's letters from all over the world arrived for Santa, I knelt on the wide stripe, painted where the Arctic Circle ran through the center of the village. I stared at the sign above: *Arctic Circle,*

Polcirkeln, Polarkreis, Circle Polaire, Napapiiri. Another post had wooden signs pointing in different directions, to places like London, New York, and Singapore. The closeness I felt with the world brought tears to my eyes. Afterward, we lunched in the cozy café and visited little shops where I bought a stuffed reindeer.

I finally arrived at Santa's office. I was really going to meet him. Upon entering, I felt foolish. Here I was, a grown woman, going to visit a fairytale character. But as soon as I saw Santa, my apprehension was replaced with childlike excitement.

He looked just as I had hoped—not tall, but not too short either. He was a little chubby, with a jolly, smiling face and a long white beard that hung nearly to his belt. Instead of the red suit, he wore brown woolen knee breeches. Under a red wool vest, his full-sleeved white wool shirt, with embroidery around the hem, hung almost to his knees. He wore soft, fur-topped brown boots.

I stared at him for a full minute before I found the courage to say, "Hello."

In English, he invited me to sit next to him on a log bench near the huge stone fireplace. His thickly accented voice was warm and friendly. He asked about my family and how I was doing.

I perched lightly on his knee for a photo, proof that I had met Santa and he was real. "Would you write a letter to my kids?" I asked.

"Ho-ho-ho! Yes," he said, patting my arm. "What do you want for Christmas?"

In my excitement, I hadn't given a thought to what I wanted. I paused to consider, then whispered my wish.

Santa nodded and winked.

I still feel the magic, the wonder, and the excitement of all the Christmas traditions. I search the nighttime Texas skies on Christmas Eve, wondering where the Star of Bethlehem is. I set out milk and cookies for Santa before I go to bed, and the glass and plate are empty in the morning.

People may laugh, but I know there's a Santa Claus because I've sat on his lap. A few Christians may think I'm being silly, but I've learned that imagination can be faith-building, necessary to grasp the truth of things we can't see. I believe the Bethlehem story, how the shepherds found the baby in a manger and the wise men brought gifts.

Maybe if we were to be more like Santa, generous in our giving, we would be more like Jesus.

By seeing his example, I believe.

Christmas Doll
by Anne Braly

Because I was born there, Brazil was the only home I knew. Growing up among the Brazilians, I was accepted. Nobody cared that my parents were American. My father was the pastor of one of the largest churches in São Paulo. After seven years on the mission field, Dad said, "We're going home for a year." He looked happy, but I wasn't. I felt like I was leaving home forever, and I wasn't sure Christmas outside the tropics could be any fun.

Our Brazilian Christmases in the 1940s centered on lively children's programs at church. I sang and played games and laughed with all my friends—so much fun that I would have gladly spent the night. I left with a paper bag of chocolates and hard candies, a rare treat. I smiled and gave hugs and said goodbye to the boys and girls like they were my cousins. Would my real relatives in America be so kind? I had my doubts.

Each Christmas in Brazil, I was ready for a new doll. After a year, my plastic doll's painted face was faded, and its limbs were dislocated from their attaching rubber-bands. My durable friend that I kept from year to year was Raggedy Andy, a doll who joined me when I went on jungle adventures with my brother Jimmy. We didn't have to go beyond our back yard to walk among huge ferns and towering trees. I wondered what Christmas in Virginia was like, where instead of rain, they had snow.

Like most of our Brazilian friends, the big celebration and gifts for ourselves came on our birthdays. Christmas was a time for celebrating the birth of Jesus, not having a party. At church, we remembered the shepherds, the wise men, and others who also celebrated His birth. At home we children received one or two small gifts.

The week after Christmas was the most fun because December in Brazil is summertime, when children are out of school and we could vacation at the beach. Jimmy and I swam and collected colorful shells on the Atlantic coast every day except Sunday.

In the evening, we joined the crowd strolling upon miles of mosaic sidewalk along the ocean. Black tiles and white tiles, laid by hand centuries ago, formed beautiful geometric designs. At the end of our walk, we stood in awe before the fountain that spewed water upward in changing colors while we made the picture permanent in our minds. As a special treat, sometimes we bought an ice-cream cone in one of our favorite flavors: coconut, avocado, or passion fruit. Would America have sandy beaches where we could play and have fun? Not in the winter.

We landed in a world that wouldn't have been stranger if Virginia had been another planet. A thick blanket covered the town of White Stone, making everything white, a sharp contrast to home where everything was green all year. I had heard descriptions, but I couldn't remember seeing snow. It was cold and slippery, but unlike the sand on the shore, I could make white balls and throw them at Jimmy. That was fun until he threw one and hit me in the face.

My widowed grandmother welcomed me, saying, "How you've grown, since I last saw you at age two." I didn't feel like I had grown. I felt like a stranger until she gave me a hug and talked to me like I was her best friend.

Unlike São Paulo with its miles of skyscrapers, the town of White Stone was a street lined with small buildings of brick, stone, and wood. The grocery store and bank were just beyond the church. Uncle Jim's hardware store was a three-block walk from the house. The people on the street were friendly, but they spoke English, not Portuguese. I wasn't sure what to say to them, so I smiled and kept walking, content to be dressed like they were, in my heavy winter coat and gloves.

When I sat at the dinner table, I wasn't sure about what I saw on my plate. I had eaten fish, but the oysters and fish eggs were something new. I would have pushed them back, saying "no thanks," but I didn't want to be treated like a foreigner. I had to accept vegetables and fruits I had never seen before, like the cranberries and blueberries.

The week before Christmas, my married brother and my sister in college came to visit. I had seen pictures, but here they were, talking to me like they had always known me. With pallets for beds, we made a place for everyone to sleep in Grandmother's small cottage.

I got to ride in my older brother's car, a real treat since all my travel in São Paulo was in streetcars or buses. When he took Jimmy and me to see a frozen pond, he assured us that we could safely walk across the ice. How was this possible? I had never imagined such a phenomenon in nature. Next, he took us to the woods where we cut down a small fir tree to decorate for Christmas.

The holidays were different from home, but I liked the feeling of peace and goodwill. In historic Williamsburg, I admired the old brick homes decorated with wreaths, candles, and Welcome signs.

In White Stone, one of Mother's childhood friends dropped by to visit her and see how her children had fared, living in Brazil. "What kind of candy do you want?" she asked me, as if she were certain my desire would be found in my Christmas stocking.

"Jellybeans," I immediately shouted. After visiting my uncle's store, they had become my favorite kind of *American* candy.

On Christmas morning, everyone gathered around the iron stove in the sitting room. To make enough space for all of us, the little tree was placed on the hat table in the entrance hallway. I couldn't believe the number of wrapped gifts, as colorful as the lights of São Paulo. I held out my arms to receive my present from the whole family, bigger than anything I had ever received before.

I carefully removed the wrapping and saved the bow. Inside, I found my constant companion who would gladly go back to Brazil with me—a baby doll with the porcelain face of an angel, with a long white dress with lace down the front. Her body was pliable, made of stuffed knitted fabric. Her porcelain hands and feet were flesh-colored, looking real. Her shiny brown eyes had black eyelashes, closing when I laid her down to sleep and opening when I picked her up.

When I returned to Brazil, my Christmas doll from America was readily accepted in my home and slept in my bedroom. My friends from school picked her up, admiring her because they had never seen an American doll before. She made friends so easily, and showed me how I could enjoy pleasant surprises, no matter where I was.

I could go to any land, from the Brazilian tropics to the cold winters of Virginia. All I had to do was relax and be friendly, like my Christmas doll.

Glitzen with Granny
by Cheryl Dawson

At Thanksgiving, I was thankful for my family, especially my two granddaughters from different families who led separate lives. I hadn't been successful in getting their parents together, but maybe I could spend time with Ashley and Serenity, who were cousins starting school, but they had never met. Was that possible? Would their personalities clash? I wouldn't know if I didn't try.

I designed a "Glitzen with Granny" invitation for each of them to spend the day with me and have "lots of fun." Puzzles were always fun. On graph paper I designed a simple find-the-words puzzle with Joseph, Mary, and Jesus. *Christmas* would be harder to find because I put it on a diagonal, running backward. Before folding the red letter-size sheet, I admired my handiwork. With script letters the layout was good enough for a wedding reception or other gala event.

When I put the invitation in the mailbox, I wondered if they would come. Of course they would. Their parents would gladly accept a free babysitter so they

187

could do things on their own. I wanted to bond with the two of them and create a Christmas memory, but how would it work? I needed a plan.

When the big day came, the cold wintry day was perfect for welcoming kids to the warmth inside. The wind blew snowflakes from the fir trees and whitened my kitchen window. The sound of feet skipping up to my door, followed by giggles, announced the arrival of my special guests. I opened the door, greeted them with a big hug, and waved goodbye to their parents.

With wide smiles of excitement, the girls jumped up and down as they saw each other for the first time.

"Look," Serenity said. "We both have long hair."

"Is it naturally curly?" Ashley asked. "I have to curl mine. What's your favorite color? Mine is pink."

"I like purple."

Well, good. At least they weren't opposites. This was a good sign.

The three of us sat around the kitchen table, drinking cups of hot chocolate sprinkled with marshmallows. After talking about how they liked school and what they planned to do during the holidays, I introduced our first project.

Being from the city, they had never made fresh butter. "Don't you think that would be fun," I asked, "making butter like I used to do on the farm?"

"Yeah!" they both said in unison.

I pointed toward my cabinet while getting a pint of heavy whipping cream from the refrigerator. "Ashley, get out that quart jar from the bottom shelf."

Ashley poured in the cream, and I tightened the lid. They had a new toy.

"Now you need to shake the jar," I said. "Be

careful not to drop it. I'll set the timer for five minutes."

"Me first," Serenity shouted, "obviously eager to see how butter was made.

As she shook the jar, I wondered where she got all that energy. She would have gone longer, but the timer sounded. She reluctantly handed Ashley the jar.

This was going well. "Isn't Glitzen with Granny fun," I said, smiling when I saw their nods.

After five more minutes, the butter was whipped into a soft, yellow ball floating on the thin milk. While I drained the butter, the girls joined hands and danced around the kitchen, chanting, "Glitzen with Granny."

I opened the oven door to let the banana and chocolate smell fill the room. "Let's have a tasty treat." We ate freshly baked banana-nut bread, spread with our freshly churned butter.

In the living room, I led them to the Christmas tree and its cedar aroma. Underneath, two gift bags each contained three Christmas storybooks, a coloring book, and a box of forty-eight crayons. "Pick out your favorite story, and I'll read it to you."

Ashley picked one she liked and curled up on the floor to listen. I was still reading the touching story that showed the value of giving when I heard a faint jingle and looked up. She was putting her silver heart necklace around Serenity's neck.

With a surprised look, Serenity said, "Thank you. I was wanting a necklace like this for Christmas."

Wonderful. Time for the next project.

"Would you like to make paperweights for your parents?" I was afraid they might say they were too grown-up for that, but they enthusiastically said yes.

Using canning jar lids for a pattern, they drew circles on Christmas fabric and glued the fabric to the bottom of the lids.

I handed them the craft jar full of marbles. "Now we need these to glue in layers on top."

Ashley screamed, "I get the red marbles!"

Serenity looked offended. "But I wanted the red ones."

While trying to create peace and joy, I had created argument and tension. From the drawer, I pulled out a toothpick and broke it in two. I held equal ends for both of them to see. "The one who draws the long piece gets the red marbles."

Serenity won and quickly picked out every last red marble. One layer at a time, the marbles were glued to the top of the lid, in three layers to make a cone.

Back in the kitchen, we baked star-shaped sugar cookies. After letting them cool on the wire rack, we dripped a tablespoon of creamy white icing over each cookie. With the same number of cookies on each of their plates, Ashley and Serenity dusted red and green sprinkles over half and put tiny gold cake-decorating balls on the rest.

On the other counter, we mixed equal amounts of fruit punch and lemon-lime carbonated soda in a large bowl. Serenity yelled, "Let's see how heavy it is."

Before I could say, "Don't try to pick it up," red punch was all over the floor. "That's okay," I said. "We can all help clean up."

With the floor mopped, it was time for lunch. I got chicken-salad sandwiches from the refrigerator. The container of spinach salad had chopped apples and mandarin oranges, sprinkled on top with dried cranberries, bacon bits, and maple-coated pecans. The holiday trail mix included chocolate candies, raisins, and peanuts. Other containers yielded a variety of home-made chocolates, fudge, and peppermint. The tiniest tins contained squares of homemade chocolate, pep-permint, and vanilla fudge drizzled with hardened chocolate.

Ashley and Serenity filled their plates and we moved into the dining room where our three places were already set on a leaf-pattern tablecloth, with matching napkins rolled into wooden Christmas hold-ers. Two large crystal bowls were filled with toys to take home.

Our tummies full, we nestled on the sofa to read the Christmas story from the Bible and talk about its importance. We were playing Christmas carols when the doorbell rang. Time for my granddaughters to go home.

Ashley hugged Serenity goodbye and whispered, "I'm glad you're my cousin."

Serenity wiped a tear from Ashley's cheek, then one of her own. "Me too!"

"Merry Christmas," I said as I kissed each one on the forehead. I wondered, *Could this be the first day of a "Glitzen with Granny" tradition?*

Christmas Two Feet Deep
by Janet Dickson

At her brother's house in Denver on the day
before Christmas Eve, Marie stared out the living room
window, wondering if the difficult drive from Texas
would be wasted. The skies were already gray, and the
forecasters predicted snow, lots of it. She had her heart
set on making wonderful memories for her four-year-
old, John, scheduled for heart surgery next month. But
if the roads were closed, her sister's family wouldn't
make it from Kansas.

Early on Christmas Eve, she got up to make coffee
and looked out the kitchen window. Oh, no! The cars
were buried in snow, at least two feet of it, and it was
still snowing so hard she could barely see across the
street. She ran to the front door and pushed, but the
door wouldn't budge.

If they couldn't dig out the cars and the roads
weren't plowed, their families wouldn't make it to
Grandma's house. She saw little hope that her sister
would be there. What could she do? First, she prayed
earnestly, trusting and believing her son would survive

heart surgery: *Lord, you've brought us this far. Make a way for us to go to the reunion. Please. For my son.*

She pushed again and the door moved, letting the snow blow in. She ran upstairs to wake everyone. "Get up!" she yelled. "We have shoveling to do before we can go to Grandma's."

Marie, her husband, her brother and his wife, and another brother took turns with two shovels until they made it to the street. While they were digging around the Jeep, Marie went to get the kids dressed. She could only hope the plows would make it through, or they weren't going anywhere.

The rumbling outside answered her prayers. The plows were busy clearing the roads.

At noon, the snow was still falling, but not heavily. Everyone piled into the Jeep, so tight they didn't need to turn on the heater. When they pulled into the driveway at Grandma's house, kids were frolicking outside the front door like they had never seen snow before—cousins from California, no doubt. They shook off the snow from making snow angels, then threw snow at one another, laughing all the time.

One of Marie's Colorado cousins threw a snowball in her direction. "A little late, aren't you? Texicans."

Marie's husband stooped to make a snowball. "You look like the abominable snowman." When pushed into a bank of snow, he came up laughing—another snowman, trying to brush the snow from his jeans.

Marie handed him the baby and helped John from the car to the ground. Her bother carried their two-year-old daughter.

Grampa yelled out the door, "Okay. That's

193

enough. Dinner's ready. Clean up or there'll be nothing left for you to eat." The smell of freshly baked bread was enough to make any snowman want to come in.

Marie led her bundled four-year-old to see her dad. "This is your Grandpa John. You have the same names." She hugged her father, drawing upon his strength.

"Look at you." Grandpa picked him up and held him high. "You're getting so big. Let's go see your great grandmother Tillie. She's been waiting all day to see you."

Gramma Tillie helped John remove his coat. "Do you remember me?" she said with a slight German accent that made Marie smile. "You came to my house in Kansas two years ago." A sweet smile broke through her wrinkles.

He took a shy step toward her.

"These are your sisters then. I bet you're a big help to Mommy with them." She looked at Marie, then to the garage where tables had been set for sixty people. "I'll take the children to dinner. You can put their stuff away in the dining room. I get tired sitting. If I can keep moving I'm all right."

The six round tables had white linen tablecloths and a Christmas tree centerpiece. From every corner of the tri-level rock home, the family filed down the garage stairs and formed a line to the buffet benches.

Waiting in line, one of Marie's aunts said, "I prayed for a white Christmas. Mark and Wendy have never seen snow before."

Another aunt said with a teasing smile, "Has it been awhile since you've prayed? God has answered you in abundance."

"Well, you know what the Bible says: the prayers of the righteous availeth much."

Marie thought, *I wish I could have some of that effective prayer for John's failing health. God, give me strength to carry on.*

Bill, the youngest of Tillie's nine remaining children, was about to finish saying the blessing when his brother said, "Amen," and heaped another spoonful of food onto his plate. When everyone was seated and eating, Marie looked at the table with ten empty chairs, where her sister's family from Kansas should be, unable to make the trip because of the weather. She smiled to cover her sadness, wondering if they were missing the one chance they had to see John. While they were sitting around, drinking coffee and eating dessert, the doorbell rang.

"I'll get it, Dad." Marie took platters to the kitchen and answered the front door. "It's Dan and his family. The Kansans are here!" She helped them hang up their coats while the rest of the family moved into the living room to greet them.

Dan stood in front of the fireplace and raised his hands. "We were so bored and it took so long to get here, we wrote a song for Grandma." They began singing to a tune that resembled "Rudolph, the Red-Nosed Reindeer."

Now there's Hays, and Topeka, Denver and Nigeria, Scottsdale, and L.A. and everywhere near ya, But do you recall, the littlest town of them all? Stratton, the snowed in city, the streets rolled up at eight. Everyone would start to snore, while snow piled high around the door. All of the other cities, used to call it names and laugh. They wouldn't let poor Stratton even get on the map.

Then one snowy Christmas eve, the Kansans made a trip.

The snow was blowing so very hard, the van would slide and slip.
All of their family loved them. Prayed for them through the night.
The Kansans drove the next day and made it to Denver all right.

Everyone clapped, cameras clicked, and lights flashed. Between blinks, with John asleep in her lap, Marie gave thanks for her family and a chance for them to see John before his heart surgery.

John opened his eyes. "Momma, I want to go home."

"We'll be home soon, son."

"No, Momma. I want to go... *home.*" He closed his eyes. Probably he meant "home to Texas," not to her brother's house. Surely he wasn't thinking about Heaven.

The snow storm hadn't prevented the whole family from getting together for a wonderful reunion. Prayer had made a difference. The same God who had kept them safe and gave them an unforgettable time together could bring John safely through heart surgery.

Giggling All the Way
by Keisha Bass

At one o'clock on Christmas morning, my sister, brother, and I tiptoed down the stairs like the Three Musketeers, wanting to make ourselves invisible. To Mom and Dad, who were busy wrapping presents, we must have more closely resembled the Three Stooges, because we couldn't keep from giggling.

Mom yelled, "Go to sleep or there'll be no Christmas in this house!"

Like six cups of coffee before breakfast, the excitement made sleep impossible. Christmas was the funnest time of the year, and I wanted those thrills to last forever.

The fun began on the day after Thanksgiving, as soon as the first decoration was put on the wall. My sister and I strung the ribbon and tinsel around the house and placed each bow. Then we hung all the cards kept from Christmases past, a reminder that peace and joy would keep coming, year after year. We opened each card, read the message inside, and used invisible tape to arrange them diagonally along the wooden rail, weaving red and silver tinsel between them.

My brother helped Dad bring the tree from the attic, grumbling about how heavy and bulky it was. As soon as the tree stood on its metal legs, my sister and I were hanging ornaments on the branches. We reached as high as our stretched-out arms and tippy toes allowed, then left the rest for Mom.

Sometime before daybreak on Christmas morning, I drifted off to sleep. I awakened when I smelled the sausage, eggs, and pancakes. The meat sizzling in the pan had worked better than any alarm.

After breakfast, Mom and Dad called our names to open presents. I raced to get one open, yelled my thanks, often with a quick kiss and hug, and moved on to the next one. The room was utter chaos. It was also a mountain of thrills.

For weeks, TV commercials and talk among the kids at school had focused on whether or not we would get a Cabbage Patch Doll. Newscasts showed frantic moms in long lines at the mall, hoping to buy one before they were gone. Could I be so lucky to get such a doll?

When I tore open the wrapping paper and saw Cherry's face, my Cabbage Patch "daughter," I felt like a mom. She came with adoption papers with her name, age, and where she was from. I would care for her—change her diapers, make sure she never missed a feeding. Wherever I went, Cherry would go too. She would love my hugs, appreciate my victories, and console my defeats.

Earlier in the morning I hadn't been that hungry, but after the gifts were all opened and the last scrap of trash was picked up, I stopped to finish off our breakfast feast before going to get dressed. When we went to my grandparents' house, we had to be dressed in our Christmas best.

My sister and I were styled from head to toe, with red ribbons in our hair and white snowballs hanging from our socks. Dad wore a red-and-green sweater with zigzag lines that would give you a headache if you stared at them for too long. Mom, in her Christmas sweater draped in jingle bells, could always be heard before you saw her. My brother's sweater was a smaller version of Dad's.

A second merry Christmas began when we pulled into my grandparents' driveway and I ran up the steps with presents under my arms. After everyone was hugged and kissed, it was time to open our gifts. I loved to see my grandparents' faces light up as they removed the bows and carefully slit the tape so the wrapping could be reused. Expressions like "Oh, my! It's beautiful," "This is perfect," and "I love it. Thank you so much," accompanied more hugs and kisses. I appreciated the gifts I received, but my biggest thrill was seeing others open their gifts.

A few years later, Mom died of cancer, and Christmas wasn't the same. I tried to imagine she was present in spirit, but her chair stood there, vacant, and no presents were marked "from Mom." As I longed for her hugs and kisses, I wiped the tears from my eyes and dearly held all that was left—my treasured memories. I could never forget the special way she made me feel at Christmas. I wanted that feeling to remain in my heart forever.

Years passed, but I wouldn't let go of our tradition. The ribbon and tinsel and pretty bows. The hanging of the Christmas cards. Some of the same ornaments I had as a child were now hanging on the Christmas tree at my house. I opened the box with all the Christmas cards I had ever received as an adult. I read each one before arranging them diagonally along the counter in the living room, hung with invisible tape. I cooked a special dinner which filled the house with the smells of Christmas. When the doorbell rang and my family came in to celebrate, I welcomed them to the same colors and smells we had enjoyed with my mom.

It was now my turn to hand out the gifts from under the red-and-silver-decorated Christmas tree. When I called each name, seeing my family's faces light up made me smile and warmed my heart.

I couldn't help but giggle a little, because I felt like Mom was there.

Christmas Is Coming
by Lyndie Blevins

Something was wrong. That was my first sensation—like trivial sounds that should have been there but weren't. "Where's Billy?" I shouted at Mom, who was studying the grocery store shelves, trying to decide which item was the best buy. How had he wandered off without my seeing him? With special needs, he wouldn't know what to do when he was lost.

I ran up the aisle, and Mom took the other direction.

I was Billy's big sister, the *responsible* one who would never let anything bad happen. A terrible thought flashed through my mind, the picture of him wandering outside, being hit by a car. I looked out the front doors but didn't see him. Down the next aisle, I took a deep breath and relaxed. He was safe, standing like a statue in front of the fresh vegetables, looking toward the ceiling, his eyes fixed on the top shelf.

Mom knelt beside him. "Billy, are you okay?"

His eyes were big and glassy, and he was taking irregular breaths like he was about to have an asthma attack. Pointing up, he whispered, "My Tiger Joe."

A big toy tank guarded the shelf above the carrots and celery, its cannon barrel big enough to catch the eye of any boy when he came through the front door. A hand-written sign said, *Tiger Joe — Remote Controlled with Missiles.*

"Why is Tiger Joe here?" Billy seemed bothered by the fact that a toy was displayed among groceries. "Why can't I touch Tiger Joe? Where are the missiles? How does Tiger Joe work?" When trying to figure out something, he asked endless questions with no pause for answers. "Does Tiger Joe fire the missiles? How far will they go? Who are the soldiers riding on Tiger Joe?" He appeared to be on the verge of tears, looking desperate and deprived. "I want my Tiger Joe."

With enough money in my piggy bank, I would have gladly bought the toy for him. But this was an expensive toy, more than my parents could afford. We walked out with only groceries, with Billy crying, "I want my Tiger Joe."

While Billy was watching television, an advertisement sounded a military cadence and showed a toy tank rolling across the screen, guided over twigs and around rocks by a boy holding a remote control. A deep voice said, "This is Tiger Joe," in a tone that said anyone who didn't have one was living an empty life. A missile came smoking from the cannon barrel. "Stop! Back! You breach load Tiger Joe and… fire!" The cannon fired three times. "Tiger Joe. Sold at food markets only."

"It's Tiger Joe," Billy said, crying. "Let's go to the store and get my Tiger Joe."

"Billy," Mom said. "It's September. Christmas is coming."

Waiting was something Billy couldn't understand. I knew what the Bible said: *Suffering produces endurance and endurance produces character and character produces hope.* No one thought Billy needed to learn suffering and endurance. He had spent most of his life enduring lingering illnesses and uncertainty. I was the one who was suffering, dying a little more inside each time my brother begged and cried.

"Christmas is coming," I said, wanting to give him hope.

By firing the canons, Billy thought Tiger Joe would keep him safe from the doctors and nurses. Adults who treated him strangely would have to back off. And the boys, who were allowed to play outside, wouldn't tease him anymore. Billy was lovable, but he couldn't handle teasing. His eyes would mist and he'd grab his chest in pain.

From the moment he woke up until his head hit the pillow, he talked about Tiger Joe. "Christmas is coming," he said proudly. "I want my Tiger Joe."

When I walked past his bedroom, I heard him talking in his sleep, saying something about Tiger Joe.

On days when Billy didn't say anything about firing cannons, I was comforted, knowing his hope for Christmas had given him peace. But he was never quiet for long. Whenever his eyes widened as though they were focusing in the distance, I knew Tiger Joe was rumbling through his mind. A trip to the store or a toy commercial on television brought a fresh chant: "Christmas is coming. I want my Tiger Joe."

In November, Mamaw picked us up at school and told us President Kennedy and a police officer had been killed not far from where we lived. After watching live television coverage of Ruby shooting Oswald, I wondered if anyone in our neighborhood was safe. Then Papaw had a heart attack, and I put my arm around Billy, thinking Christmas would never be the same. Would Billy get his Tiger Joe? I didn't want to see him cry.

On December twenty-first, Mamaw and Papaw came to live with us. Everyone believed having his family with him was the best medicine for his recovery. I was warned not to cause any excitement that might put a strain on Papaw's heart, but there was no way to keep Billy from saying, "Christmas is coming. I want my Tiger Joe."

How would we handle Santa coming? I imagined how much noise Billy would make, with shrieks and shouting, "My Tiger Joe!" Mom made special arrangements for Mamaw and Papaw to wait for Santa on Christmas Eve while the rest of us were out looking at Christmas lights. I was the only one who thought seeing Santa would be too much excitement for Papaw's heart.

"Quiet," Mom said as we returned. "Don't get Papaw too excited."

I took a deep breath, which put me behind Billy in running into the living room, to a bounty of gifts left by Santa. The gigantic Tiger Joe was in the center of all the gifts. I sighed, relieved that my suffering was over. I expected Billy to go straight to Tiger Joe, but he didn't. Apparently his focus on everything he hadn't seen before had caused him to miss what was most obvious.

Billy looked at a smaller gift on the left, then ran around the tank like it wasn't there, to look at a gift on the other side of the tree. When he saw the tank, he screamed, "My Tiger Joe!" and jumped up and down, his face radiant with joy. He kept shouting, "I got it! I got my Tiger Joe."

Christmas had finally come.

Hollywood Christmas
by Pam Lewiston

In a neighborhood where tourists and celebrities came in luxury cars, wearing fancy clothes, eating in expensive restaurants, I rose from my sleeping spot in the alley and sneezed to clear the dust from my nostrils. Holiday music was already blaring from the nearby shops, inviting customers. I wasn't buying. I was looking for a way to survive the day.

My fellow sleeping companions stirred. What an odd mixture of youth I had joined—freedom-loving hippies, drugged-out zombies, and runaways—people who were more fearful of their homes than the swollen streets. I didn't belong here, but I had nowhere else to go.

I snatched my pillowcase of belongings and ran to the nearest gas station to wash. As soon as I was alone in the restroom, I reached into my knee-high moccasins. Just a few coins—not even a dollar to get something to eat. I needed a job. How could I survive?

One of the girls from the alley barged in. "Peace. How long you been on your own?" She untangled her

206

long blond hair, washed her face, and stared at me, waiting.

"Couple of months." I backed toward the door.

She smiled and stepped closer, blocking my exit. "You can panhandle with me today, if you want."

"What's that?"

"How square. It's how you get bread, sister. Money." She laughed and slapped the wall. "You spaz. "You're going to d-i-e out here."

I returned to the alley, now vacant, and sank to the ground. Her words stung. She was right. I was a retard. I had to do something, but what? I could pimp myself out, but I didn't like that idea. I leaned against the brick wall and closed my eyes to think. What options had I missed?

"You look bummed out?" A man's slurred voice. "Coming down?"

"Don't sweat it, dude. Trying to chill." I opened my eyes. "Bug out. I don't trip."

"Far out. Don't lose your cool. I'm gone." He staggered down the alley.

A brisk stroll carried me to Grauman Chinese Theater where tourists flowed out of their buses. They pushed one another aside to take pictures and place their hands and feet into the imprints in the concrete. I melded with the group, keeping eager eyes for a coin that might drop from a child's hand or from adults bending over. Two hours and a measly eighty-one cents later, I felt light-headed. I needed to eat. I should have stayed with the bathroom hippie.

The smell of corned beef and fresh bread drew me down the street like a grizzly to a stream leaping with salmon. Through the window of Brown's Confectionary, I watched the balding man pack boxes of Christmas goodies. I drooled with each piece of candy he placed in the box. After removing my knit beanie, I fluffed my hair and tried to iron my skirt with my hands. I dry-brushed my hair and ran my tongue over my teeth.

The man looked up when the bell sounded and I walked in. "What may I do for you?"

I lowered my head to escape his piercing eyes that seemed all-knowing. "Umm... How much is one of your sandwiches?"

"Without any side, $1.25. Drinks are a quarter."

The store was empty, but I whispered, "Would you sell half a sandwich?"

He smiled as he pointed to the display. "What would you like?"

"Just half a corned beef, please."

Three minutes later, I had a whole corned beef on rye sitting in front of me, with a glass of water and a soda. I didn't like the man staring at me. Did he think I was a social oddity? I bowed my head, not to pray, but to avoid his gaze. I wolfed down the first half of my sandwich without looking up. The food was too satisfying to care about table manners.

With my stomach full, no longer rumbling like an earthquake, I wrapped the remainder and slipped it into my pocket. While sipping my drink, I watched customers come and go, taking a break from shopping or a movie. Seeing sleepy toddlers snuggled in their parents' arms made me homesick.

When the owner approached, I stood. "Thank you for your kindness."

"You're welcome. If you're interested in work,

come by tomorrow. I may have something."

Stone-like, I stared at him, mumbling. "Thank you. What time?"

"Around nine."

That night I toured Hollywood Boulevard and dreamed of home. The festive decorations reminded me of the flocked tree, tinsel, and lights—and the presents underneath. I window-shopped, imagining what I would buy for my sister and two brothers—something that would be a thrilling surprise. One day, because I had a job, I could afford such gifts.

At work the next day, Brown's Confectionary was flooded with business from the Hollywood Christmas Parade. I was exhausted.

As we closed, Mr. Schumacher said, "I'll walk you."

"No need, sir." I headed for the door. "I'm just down the street."

He put his hand on my shoulder. "No, I'll walk you. Where are you parked?"

What could I say to keep him from knowing what a liar I was? "Oh… umm… I just have to wait for the bus."

"No need. I'll drive you to your place."

He had driven only five blocks when I said, "Up there. You can drop me in front of that apartment building." I thanked him, ran inside, and waited for him to leave before taking my spot in the alley.

A week later, Mr. Schumacher was speaking with one of our regular customers, the manager of the apartment building next door. I couldn't hear what they were saying, but I had never seen Mr. Schumacher so animated before. When he glanced toward me, I turned away. Soon after that, he said to me, "I want to talk with you after work."

What had I done wrong? I wanted to run and hide. Nothing good could come from this conversation. I prepared for the worst. I would be fired.

After hours, he sat across from me in the booth where I had eaten my first sandwich, smiling like he had something good for me. "The manager of the building next door has a basement apartment for you. There's no deposit, and you can stay free for one month. After that, he expects monthly rental payments."

Speechless, I stared at him for a minute, tears filling my eyes. "Why?"

Mr. Schumacher told me about God's love, how he'd been helped and forgiven many times. "It's getting cold," he said, "and you need a place to stay. Everyone needs a hand up once in a while."

That night, I sat on the twin bed and thought about the meaning of peace on earth, goodwill toward men. Other than the bed, one tiny table, and a chair, the room was bare. A single light bulb lit the room. The bathroom was down the hall, but I felt like I had a room in a palace.

Because of God's love and forgiveness, a Christian came bearing gifts. That's what it takes to have a true Hollywood Christmas.

Christmas Assignment
by Al Speegle

Twas a day before his paper was due and all through the night, Jamie Washington turned restlessly in bed, churning nightmares.

I'm sorry, the coach said in a tone so real that Jamie thought he was awake. *You flunked your English class. You can't play basketball.*

With a jerk, he pushed up from his pillow and looked at the clock: 3:00 a.m. What day was it? Oh, Sunday, and he still hadn't started his writing assignment. He could hear his eighth-grade teacher's voice: *Write three pages on "The Best Christmas I Ever Had." It's due on Monday.*

Jamie couldn't think of any Christmas worth remembering. He couldn't go back to sleep, worried that whatever he wrote wouldn't be good enough to let him play ball. At the breakfast table, he stirred his oatmeal while staring out the window.

"What's up with you?" Mom asked.

"Oh, I've got to write this paper for school. Have I ever had a Christmas when I got something other than

211

a candy bar and maybe a shirt or something?"

"Like what, some fancy electronic thing you know we can't afford? You should be thankful we still have a roof over our heads. If this weren't a government project, we'd have been kicked out for being three months late on payments."

"I know, but I've got to write something." His bite of oatmeal tasted like cardboard, but that was better than nothing. "I might not"—he cut himself off, deciding not to tell her that he couldn't play basketball—"I mean, I'll think of something."

He pulled paper from his notebook, stretched out on the bed, and began to write:

Maybe it weren't the best Christmas, but it's the first one I remember. I can still see Granny there in front of the poinsettia wreath. Sittin in her rockin chair. Tears wet on her cheeks. Maybe she knowed where she was goin, cause she had just gone and died. Momma said she was in Heaven, but I don't know how she could tell. Momma cried a lot.

It was the week after Pappa got released from prison. I thought we'd finally get to be a happy family like I seen on TV. I don't know where he was when Granny went to Heaven. When he come home Momma and him got in this big fight. Before he fell asleep Pappa told me he seen Santa and that's why he got home so late. Next mornin Momma said he had too much Christmas spirits.

Christmas morning Pappa overslept. Said he had the midnight flu. We didn't get any presents. Momma said Santa didn't show up cause he got lost. Easy to do in our neighborhood.

The teacher said three pages. How could he write that much? If he didn't put something down, he was sure to get an F, so he told about the time Pappa fished Christmas lights out of the dumpster, got them to

212

working, and then fell off the upstairs patio and broke his leg while trying to put them up.

Jamie turned to page two and kept writing.

That was the year Momma said she heard on the radio Santa got mugged on 54th street. All our presents was stolen. He sent a letter of apology. Said he'd make it up to us. I was so proud of his letter I showed it to the kids at school. They said Santa didn't exist, that our parents buyed the gifts. I asked Momma 'bout that. Santa was at one store, and when we went to another store, there he was again. Momma said they were just working for Santa. The real Santa was at the North Pole, bein sure the toys was made. So now I know the truth and it don't matter what kids say.

Jamie wrote about the next year, when Momma wrapped oatmeal raisin cookies with shiny Christmas paper for the needy kids at church. He described the magic scissors, how they curled the ribbon when the strands were pulled across the blade. He remembered Mom singing, which made him anticipate a merry Christmas until what happened after that.

On Christmas Eve our apartment caught fire. Momma said Pappa passed out on the sofa with a lit cigarette. Again. Lots of smoke. We all made it out alive, but my best friend next door died. His brother was shot in a drive by on New Year's Eve.

Two weeks later, my brother joined the Army. He was happy to be getting out of the hood. See the world. Have a chance to get a college education. I was proud of him for making our country safe. He was my hero. I wanted to be just like him when I growed up. He wrote me a letter. Said there were lots of heroes, not just him. He sent pictures of him on a beach in California, some with him and his girlfriends in Japan, Korea, and Germany. Next to my bed I kept the picture of him with his buddies next to a helicopter.

213

On the third page, Jamie wrote about the following year, when his sister gave birth to twins on Thanksgiving day. They were so sure this Christmas would be a happy time, but Momma in her wisdom said some days we have sunshine and other days we have storms.

On Christmas Eve a car stopped in front of our apartment. I called Momma to the window. Two men dressed in uniforms walked up our sidewalk. Momma started screaming. Folk from the church came and prayed with her, but she didn't feel no better. They never opened the casket. Everybody knew he was in there cause of my brother's picture on top. Someone played a trumpet while heroes folded the flag. One of them handed the flag to Momma and said, "With thanks from a grateful nation." Then he saluted her.

On Monday at his second-period English class, Jamie handed his paper to the teacher, resigned to the fact that he wouldn't be playing basketball. Not this season. His momma praying that he'd make an A wasn't going to help. He knew his grammar was bad, and he hadn't really done the assignment. He wrote the best he could, but it wasn't about "The Best Christmas I Ever Had."

The next day, he was dreaming about being off for the holidays when the teacher handed him his graded paper. A big letter A was circled at the top, and a note: *You have a wonderful gift for writing from the heart. Well done.*

Jamie didn't shout, *Yes! I'm going to play basketball.* He avoided making a show, but he was thinking, *This is the best Christmas I ever had.*

Proud With Red-and-Green
by Dorothy Ward-Winters

I love Christmas with its colorful lights and joyful songs.

In 1947, the season was a refreshing escape from the years of low wages and war-time rationing. Daddy's new job in Fort Worth gave me hope that gifts this year would be more than peppermint candy, a trinket, or pajamas. I wouldn't be embarrassed to tell my class-mates what I got for Christmas.

A post-war bomb dropped when I learned that Mother had been diagnosed with tuberculosis, a lung disease acquired when she was a child and an infected uncle came to live with her family. Tuberculosis can lie dormant for years. In her case, the full-blown disease came after thirty years. After learning that her chances of recovery were good, I still worried. Her treatment called for complete bed rest in a sanitarium until she was cured, which could take many months, maybe a year or more. Who would take her place, doing the baking and shopping that made Christmas so special?

Mother pleaded with the doctors. "I can't stay

away from home. I have young children. I need to be there every day even if I'm in bed. I promise I'll stay in bed. Just let me stay be with my children."

The county health society agreed to her request. Mother was bed-ridden at home, unable to do anything other than give instructions on what was needed. She ate from special dishes that were boiled after each use. Daddy kept her bedroom as clean and sterile as possible, with a bath towel and washcloth reserved for her exclusive use. I joined my brothers and sister doing housework and tending the farm animals.

When school began in the fall, I knew there was no hope for Mother getting out to Christmas shop. Our home was quarantined. We attended church and school, but we had strict instruction to keep our distance from Mother.

"Don't kiss her or hug her," Daddy said. "Don't go into her bedroom."

Everybody at school—all the teachers, students, and staff—had to be tested for tuberculosis. This was my fault. Teachers tried to console me, but I still felt responsible.

Mother couldn't join us at the table. Christmas would be especially tough, her favorite time of the year, when she wouldn't get to bake her special cornbread dressing, pecan pie, and fruitcake.

Daddy wore an apron well, perhaps because Mother gave good instructions about what to do in the kitchen. He could handle cooking, but I had my doubts about his ability to shop for Christmas. Buying for the boys wouldn't be a problem, but how would he know what to get me and my sister? He had no idea what sizes, colors, and styles of clothes we liked.

216

"Honey," he said to Mother, "What can I get the girls?"

"A dresser set with hair brush and comb would be nice," she said. "Girls always brush their hair before going to bed."

Dresser set? What was a dresser set? I knew, but Daddy wouldn't know, and he wasn't one to ask directions. On Christmas morning, I would find a wrapped package under the tree, and it would probably have something to do with my hair. Whatever it was, I hoped it would be nice enough that I could proudly describe it to my friends at school.

The bright Christmas morning made the frost glisten white on the lawn. Outside the window, icy crystals drifted down like tiny snowflakes, sparkling in the sunlight. With high expectations, I joined my sister and brothers around the tree in the living room, facing Mother's bedroom door. She watched from her bed, propped up against the headboard, dressed in her finest bed jacket.

When I opened my present, I stared at the box in disbelief. A spool of ribbon. Not ribbon for my hair either. This was Christmas gift-wrapping ribbon, red-and-green, colors I would never put in my hair. I glanced at my sister, who had a puzzled look, holding ribbon just like mine.

Daddy was smiling like we should be happy with what he had picked out for us. I smiled back and said, "Thank you, Daddy." I spoke in my most sincere tone. I didn't have the heart to show my disappointment, not when his expression clearly showed how much he loved us. My sister joined me in thanking Daddy, but I could tell she was confused. How would I explain this to the

217

kids at school?

On my first day back at school, I went straight to my classroom, avoiding any chance of someone asking what I got for Christmas.

Mrs. Smith smiled like today's class would be something special. "Did everybody have fun during the holidays?" She looked around the room, gratified by the positive nods and students saying yes. "Let's go around the room so everybody can tell what they got for Christmas."

I wanted to say, *I think I have tuberculosis*, but the kids would know I wasn't sick. I wanted to go to the restroom, but the class had just started. That excuse wouldn't work. As students took their turns, I kept asking, *What am I going to say?* The other kids described their coats and sweaters, dresses and blue jeans, balls and bats, while I sat in agony. Did they really get all that expensive stuff, or were they stretching the truth?

I could never get away with lying. I might fool the teacher, but the kids would see my face and know. I didn't want to say I got red-and-green ribbon used to wrap presents. Somehow I needed to tell the truth without including the parts that would make me ashamed and embarrass my family.

My turn came before I was ready, so I spoke on impulse more than plan. "My daddy did the Christmas shopping this year. He found this special ribbon he knew I would like. I love ribbons in my hair. I have a color to match every dress I own. Now I have so much ribbon I can even decorate the mirror in my bedroom. I am very proud of my ribbons, but I'm proudest of my daddy who is taking care of us while Mother is sick."

Silence.

Do they know I'm not telling the whole story? I looked for approval, but all I saw were shocked expressions, as if the kids were thinking, *I wish I had said that.*

By not telling a lie, I forced myself to find the deeper truth. Our home had caring parents who loved the Lord. One day, Mother would keep house again and spread delicious meals on the table. And she would do the Christmas shopping.

This was Daddy's year to show the depth of his love, which was the greatest gift of all. He didn't buy pink ribbon for my hair, but he made me proud with red-and-green.

Never More Stranger
by Barbara Ferguson

When you've lived to arrive
At the age of seventy-five,
There is much to remember
From every December.

My senior-year Christmas, Len gave me a ring.
He claimed he hadn't meant to give me that thing.
He invited me to shop at a jewelry store
For a nice pen set, but nothing more.

The six childless years while Len was in school,
Giving mission gifts to Jesus seemed a good rule.
But when our five-year-old niece came to stay
A new plan was needed for Christmas Day.

How could a child learn about God and believing
Without something tangible for giving and receiving?
We each took her shopping and let her pick out
A gift while explaining what God's Gift was about.

We never knew how long she would be there,
But we purchased Sara her own little chair.
We bought her a phonograph with her favorite song,
And a chalkboard for drawing, and she drew all day
    long.

Our Santa intentions took an unfortunate turn.
It appeared these new parents had so much to learn.
The phonograph stayed silent with no needle in it.
She was allergic to chalk, and got sicker by the minute.

But she rocked in her chair by the low coffee table
Looking at the manger scene that didn't have a stable,
Which she had created from an old oatmeal box,
Baby Jesus on grass, wrapped up in her socks.

Old plastic bottles she had used as the base
For Mary and Joseph, each with a hand-painted face
On baby-food-jar heads with hand-crafted clothes.
She recited the Baby Jesus story she knows.

The next year she painted a mural for the wall
With shepherds and wise men, star, stable, and all.
Not wanting a repeat of last year's catastrophe,
We wanted a gift she'd enjoy under the tree.

How long could it take for a dolly bunk bed?
It's an "easy-to-assemble" gift, the box said.
So Santa and his helper stayed up really late
And ate all the cookies Sara left on the plate.

The next year we welcomed a sweet baby boy
Who reminded us all of the first Christmas joy.
The seasonal decorations needed to be modified
With toy animals and blocks. Bethlehem was simplified.

A couple of years later Christmas seemed rather lonely.
Sara had gone home, leaving our two sons only.
By now we were living in our own little home
With space for a big tree and a large yard to roam.

In the hills of Ohio, trees often need thinning,
So our family could cut down the tree we'd be
    trimming.
For four years Clyde lived with us and helped trim the
    tree.
At six-foot-four, he put the star on top easily.

The year Len had the brain tumor really was sad.
The boys went to the hospital to be with their dad.
The next year was harder without him at all,
But we spent it with cousins, so the boys had a ball.

We moved to New Mexico and joined a big church.
Steve and Dave got solos in the musical search.
We often spent Christmas with cousins far away
Or with grandparents so we wouldn't be alone Christ-
    mas Day.

One Christmas vacation, quarantined with the mumps,
The neighborhood boys didn't want us down in the
    dumps,
They played in our house from morning till night
And helped paint the boys' bedroom. Oh, what a sight!

When Grandpa remarried there were cousins their age,
So football on Christmas became all the rage.
It was even better with snow on the ground.
They could get soaking wet with mud all around.

Years later when the boys were married and away,
I would often visit in their home on Christmas Day.
The water pipes froze the year Steve had some guests,
So we caroled friends with empty jars and ice chests.

When grandchildren were little, it always was fun
To watch them play with the boxes when unwrapping
    was done.
As they grew older, their traditional stunt
Was to find their big present on a long treasure hunt.

When I retired, I moved close to my son.
With three young grandchildren, Christmas was fun.
There were school programs: singing, drama, and
    bands.
We always were busy with holiday demands.

Now I enjoy Christmas by Steve's fireplace
Where stockings are hung and the children all race
To see who will be Santa and who'll read The Story.
It's hard with such treasures to give God all the glory.

A family tradition we all like real well
Is cinnamon rolls baking—what a wonderful smell!
Once we tried a new recipe the day before,
But dough overflowed when we opened the fridge
    door.

Last year the church children put on a play
That showed how people misunderstand what we say.
Frankenstein and Myrtle came following the star
Instead of wise men bringing precious gifts from afar.

A few Christmases were normal, but more often
    stranger,
But none as unusual as God's Son in a manger.
Our circumstances don't determine our joy
Or our worth or our peace—gifts of that First Christ-
    mas Boy.

The Perfect Gift
by George Dalton

The first Christmas after my wife, Jean, and I were married, I desperately wanted to please her. We didn't have much money. I was working part-time for a big commercial bakery so I could complete my college education. Jean was working all day in an office in downtown Dallas, but our checks combined were barely enough to pay the bills and my tuition. Buying something expensive, like diamond earrings, was more than what I could afford to dream about. What could I do?

I felt guilty about Jean working fulltime so I could go to school. I wasn't carrying my share of the financial burden. I was desperate. It was Christmas, a time for gifts and expressions of love. I tried to think of something special, but I couldn't think of anything suitable.

The perfect opportunity was right in front of me. I just needed several days to see it. Because I worked in a bakery, I had the formula to make tens of thousands of delicious Christmas cookies. With simple math to reduce the batch size, I could show my love with a beautiful tray of cookies still hot out of the oven when Jean got home. I would also demonstrate my superb baking skills.

"Formula" was the all-important word. I had the ideal ingredients for the perfect gift. After carefully doing the math, I wrote down the recipe. The minute I got home from school, I pulled the largest bowl from the cabinet, mixed the correct ingredients in the specified amounts, and left the dough to rise while I went to the living room to study.

An hour later, I laid my textbook aside, stretched, and walked back to the kitchen to finish baking my platter of cookies. I stopped in the doorway and gasped. Like something out of a science-fiction movie, a giant mushroom had grown out of the mixing bowl and was taking over the room.

I trimmed off huge chunks from the sides of the bowl and the kitchen cabinet, rolled the dough flat, and stamped out cookies—enough to fill one cookie sheet, then another. I popped them into the oven. I had dough left over, and the mushroom was still rising. I kept cutting and stamping out little angels, bells, and trees.

Someone at the bakery had told me I could dust white flour over the dough to keep it from rising. In a hurry, I splattered white flour over the mushroom, leaving a dusting over the kitchen counter. No, it was more like a seventy-mile-per-hour West Texas dust storm, coating the floor and every other horizontal surface in the kitchen. And the mushroom was still growing.

Not to be defeated, I kept pulling trays from the oven and baking more angels, bells, and trees until I ran out of places to put the fresh-baked cookies. The whole house smelled like a bakery. It looked like one too, as I spread platters of cookies on the dining room table and searched for more space. Holding one platter, I stepped on Cleo, our cat, which sent cookies sailing, raised a cloud of white dust, and left Cleo screaming as she flew out the cat door.

In a panic, I prayed, "Help me, Jesus." On second thought, maybe I didn't want that prayer. Wasn't Jesus the one who multiplied the loaves and fish to feed a multitude? I needed to think smaller, not bigger.

When Jean walked into the kitchen from the garage, I knew she was impressed. The look on her face made sharp contrast with everything white. "What in the world happened?" she asked.

"I've been baking," I said, covered in flour.

"Yes, I can see that." She was smiling, but I couldn't tell whether her expression was from surprise or traumatic shock.

"Things didn't turn out exactly as I expected." I wiped the flour from my eyes, thinking I had just made the understatement of the century.

The house did smell good, and we had Christmas cookies for our friends and relatives, everyone at church, and all the hungry kids in China. I used all my next pay check from the bakery to purchase tin gift boxes to put the cookies in. After three weeks, Jean coaxed Cleo back into the house with the promise that Daddy would stay out of the kitchen. Even then, Cleo hissed at me whenever I walked by, in cat talk saying she would be telling all her cat friends and progeny to watch out for me.

People said my cookies were good. Dunked in hot chocolate, they were even better, but I couldn't recommend them for breakfast, lunch, and dinner.

227

I felt bad that I hadn't found the perfect gift, but Jean encouraged me. "Why don't you put up the Christmas tree?" she asked. "The house needs more lights outside. Have you finished reading that book?"

I'm sure Jean wanted me in the kitchen, but there was never any time. There was always something else I needed to do.

"You've been working too hard," she said. "You should relax and listen to Christmas carols."

Many years later, I'm still looking for that perfect gift.

Christmas Challenge
by Gloria Ashby

My mind wasn't on work when the senior executive brought me the assignment. Thoughts about time off for shopping, wrapping packages, and baking disappeared. Was he crazy? In a few weeks, how could I accomplish what a national team had worked on for months and only improved?

I appreciated his confidence in me. This was my chance to prove my skills and earn a place among senior management. But the deadline was impossible. I felt trapped, as if I were snowbound and had no way to get there.

It was my turn to host our family gathering, and I hadn't finished decorating. Now I might not have the time. I had to say yes to the project because I couldn't say no, but what if I failed? I took a deep breath, trying to calm myself. *Go home. Think about it overnight. Put together a plan.* Part of me wanted to believe, but the project couldn't be completed before Christmas. No way. How could my boss believe it could be?

I needed a team with the right skills, but who was

available and qualified to help? Nearly everyone, including me, scheduled vacation time around the holidays. I couldn't think of anyone. Even after Christmas, if I could get the deadline extended, we faced the New Year's crunch when all our time and resources were focused on surviving our busiest month of the year.

Neither the twinkle of Christmas lights nor the icy air that promised a rare snowfall in Texas lifted my spirits as I drove home. All the Yuletide cheer and thoughts of fun-filled parties were gone. Hopelessness had a strangling grip around my throat. What if I failed? I'd prove I wasn't bright enough, skilled enough, or well-connected enough to be a senior manager.

At home, sequestered from office distractions, I mulled over a starting point and the best potential team members. After a long night of planning, sorting through every possibility I could think of, I sketched out a draft of next steps. By morning, I had visions of success, but the deadline haunted me.

Facing a Herculean task, I trudged into work feeling overwhelmed.

An image popped into my head, followed by the thought: *You should call Dawn.* I argued against the idea, unsure where it had come from. *Why would you not call her?* She was a capable team player, having been my partner on several previous projects. She might at least provide some perspective on this initiative.

While dialing her number I was thinking, *I'll bounce a few ideas off her—if she hasn't cut out for Christmas yet.*

Dawn answered on the first ring.

With a hint of sarcasm, I silently mouthed a prayer: *Well, thank you, Lord, for this small gift.* While I laid out my proposal, Dawn listened patiently.

"So what do you think?" I held my breath, half expecting to hear her laugh and say, "You want to do what by when? Are you kidding? You should give up now."

"You're right on track," she said. "In fact, I'm so pleased you thought to call me. I worked on this very issue about a year ago, but I never got any traction."

"Really?" I tried to sound pleased and not totally shocked at her response. Had Dawn handed me a miracle that would meet the deadline?

"I still have my notes," she said. "I don't want to be presumptuous, but would you mind if I worked with you on this?"

I pulled the receiver away from my ear and stared at it, not believing what it was saying. Did Dawn actually say what I thought she said? She already had the groundwork laid, and now she wants to help me finish the job. Had God led me to a solution that I would never have found on my own?

Thank you, I said, grateful to God that I hadn't ignored my thought to call her. Then I realized I still had Dawn on the phone, waiting for my response.

"Why, uh, y-yes... Of course." I stuttered and stammered, still stunned at what had just happened. "Absolutely. I had... I mean, I was hoping you were available to join the project team."

For the next five minutes, we finalized our plans. Still addled by the conversation, I fumbled the receiver back into its cradle. Was this a coincidence, or was I being led in a direction I could never have planned, like the wise men who followed the star? Maybe the wisest choice I could make was following God's lead.

The scene recorded by Matthew suddenly had

231

deeper meaning. The wise men didn't have everything figured out when they left the Far East. They had to follow the star. In Jerusalem, they sought the newborn king and learned from Scripture to go to Bethlehem, where they found the child, their guiding star shining above the rooftop. They followed the leading of a dream, returning home another way, avoiding King Herod. For the whole journey, their wisdom was in following God, because they couldn't be sure of their plan.

Jesus said he was the way, and we needed to follow him. As I reviewed the story of his birth, peace and joy warmed my weary soul. I could trust him to light my path, to guide me through any difficulty, large or small. With his help, I could meet any challenge, even during the Christmas season.

With God, all things are possible if I will follow the star that shows me the way.

Snow Globe
by Jacqueline Hannah

I pushed up my collar and pulled my scarf tighter. Cold weather in Maine was normal, but not the bare ground, not for Christmas. My young sons were disappointed. I felt sad for them, determined to somehow make the week memorable before we moved to the deep South where we would never see snow for the holidays.

Wind swept down from the forested hill into our tiny New England town's main street. Holiday decorations, tied at each lamppost, flapped in the stiff breeze. The silver and red bells, candy canes, and angels shouted that Christmas would soon arrive, but the gray, bare streets denied the season's existence.

"Where's the snow, Mom?" Mathew asked.

My thoughts moved from the dull surroundings and focused on Mathew and Ben. "My thoughts exactly." I knelt down, snuggled each stocking cap lower, and helped them with their mittens. "It sure doesn't feel like Christmas, does it?"

The three of us searched the sky, hoping to see a

233

cloud somewhere. "Not gonna happen," I said. "I don't see clouds anywhere, and Christmas is only a few days away. I'm sorry." We continued our walk to the park.

"But it has snowed every Christmas since we came here." Ben kicked at the brown dirt. "It's gotta snow for our last one." He scuffed his way to the playground, then jumped into the first open swing.

Another burst of wind scurried brown leaves along the walking path. The crusty, brown objects had long ago lost their bright red, orange, and yellow colors of fall and should be covered with snow by now. They swirled and flew up in different directions. Their antics reminded me of last year's holiday storm, when the swirling, blowing snow stacked higher than we had ever thought was possible. The thermometer dropped to thirty degrees below zero and remained there for a whole month. This winter had been warmer, but was plenty cold enough for snow if the clouds would come our way.

"Hey, Mom!" Mathew called from high in the swing. "Remember the tunnels we built for the dogs last year?"

I remembered. We called the high-walled open-top paths we cleared for doggie potty-runs "tunnels," which made the clearing process more fun.

"I liked the igloos the big kids made best of all," Ben said.

Now that was fun. Driveway and sidewalk shoveling became a means to an end—an igloo village, complete with a hot chocolate café.

A strong rush of cold wind grabbed at my scarf and brought me back to our barren landscape. Mathew pumped his legs to lift himself upward. Ben was catching up.

"Higher, push us higher," Mathew said.

Both boys pushed forward and leaned back with all their strength, straining to outdo each another. They didn't need my help, but I maneuvered behind them and gave each one a good shove anyway.

A shift in the wind led me to check the sky. High clouds were moving in from the north, not the kind of clouds that would bring snow, just a further reminder of what we were missing. The persistent gale snatched away the boys' laughter. Bare branches clicked together while small evergreens bowed and whispered, saying it was time to go home.

"Come on, boys." I clapped my gloved hands. "Let's make some cocoa."

They jumped from their swings onto the hard, crusted mud. Ben stared at the ground. "Everything's brown," he said.

Mathew leaned back, hands cupped to his mouth, and shouted at the sky. "Please, God. Let it snow for our last Christmas in Maine."

I wanted to say amen. Wouldn't that be nice if God would ride in and save the day? But there wasn't much chance of that. I had seen the forecast. "Snow would be nice," I said, "but we need to be thankful, no matter what comes our way."

Christmas Eve arrived with dull gray skies and plenty of excitement. "The weatherman said it might snow," Ben said. To him, that meant a white Christmas for sure.

"Don't get your hopes up," I said. "A 10 percent chance isn't enough to make a snowman."

At least once every hour, the boys pressed their

noses against the cold window until the fog wouldn't let them see out. Nothing. The sky was gray, but snowflakes weren't falling. The ground remained brown.

The last *Amen* at the Christmas Eve service saw the backs of my boys as they raced out the church doors. Both of them returned with long faces, shaking their heads.

I herded them to our Suburban.

Mathew hopped into the backseat next to his brother and balanced a package on his lap. "I can't wait 'til we get to Candy and Brett's. Their house always smells so good."

Before starting the car, I turned to look back. "Do we have everything?" The bright-colored packages adorned with sparkling ribbons and bows balanced themselves across the back seat. The warm bread and cinnamon smelled delicious.

Our last Christmas Eve with friends in New England required some travel time. Even though the trek occurred over dry roads and bridges, the holiday spirit welcomed us as we pulled into their drive. A single candle glowed in each window. Evergreen boughs and red bows were wrapped around the home's front columns and door, making the New England tradition come alive for us.

A breeze nipped at my nose as we clamored from the car's warmth into the night air. I wrapped my scarf closer. We grabbed armloads of packages and walked down the drive toward the back door. Something cold and wet fluttered against my eyelash and onto my cheek.

"Hey, boys. Look, it's snowing."

Sure enough, a few big flakes were drifting down.

236

The boys dropped their packages and chased each flake. In the next three minutes, Mathew covered every inch of the front yard as he ran to catch the next flake and watch it melt on his mitten. "Snow!" he shouted. "It's going to be white for Christmas. Thank you, God."

"Watch this." Ben ran with his mouth open to capture a floating flake on his tongue.

After everyone had come inside, I was ready for hot chocolate and opening presents. Not the kids. They were making plans for tunnels and igloos. I smiled, questioning the wisdom of such lavish plans based on a few snowflakes.

Our midnight ride home left tracks on powdered bridges and roads. Deep footprints marked our walk from our garage to the front door.

Our final Christmas didn't provide enough snow for igloos and tunnels. That came later. But whenever I see a snow globe turned upside-down and righted again, I remember our last Christmas in Maine.

Chef's Surprise
by Gail Morris

Working in the kitchen was not my idea of fun. Before I was married, I told my fiancé how it would be. "I don't cook," I said. And I meant it until I realized how much I might gain if I could impress my in-laws with my culinary skills.

"I want to host our families for a big Christmas dinner," I said.

"Seriously?" My husband must have wondered what kind of feast could be served on burnt toast.

"Yes, I want your family to feel welcome in our home. If I organize and plan everything, it will be the perfect day."

He looked skeptical but impressed. My plan was already working.

No way I could do this by myself. Whenever I was desperate, I knew who to call. I phoned my mother and begged for help. After telling her my plan, I waited for instructions.

Silence. I thought we'd been disconnected.

She chuckled. "Are you sure?"

"Absolutely. I want a meal just like you would cook. Traditional turkey and ham. Green beans. Yams with marshmallows. Mashed potatoes with gravy, of course."

After we put together a list of everything I wanted to serve, she dictated a detailed grocery list and told me where to find the recipes.

I had a cookbook but never used it. I stared at the two pages of items I needed from the grocery store and asked myself, *What have I gotten myself into?*

I asked my in-laws to bring their favorite dishes, which was sure to give the final, perfect touch to my spread of tasty delights.

One week before Christmas, I braved the crowded store. As the items piled up, I felt more and more like a chef. By the time I reached the checkout counter, the cart looked like a dump truck—filled to the brim and ready to tip over.

When I emptied my car, I wished for a cart. Grocery sacks covered my entire kitchen counter, but with my natural attention to detail, I knew I could do this. I arranged ingredients according to each menu item. Marshmallows, Karo syrup and brown sugar by the yams. Rosemary and sage by the package of corn-bread mix. I even grouped the refrigerated items.

I taped my menu and recipes to the cabinet door and determined which items could be prepared before the big day. Nobody liked room-temperature meat, lukewarm veggies, or rolls served ten minutes late. Everything needed to be perfectly timed.

On Christmas Eve our house buzzed with activity. The centerpiece accented the china plates with red-berried holly. Mulberry candles waited to be lit, and the green crystal goblets were clean and sparkling. I placed the pristine sterling silverware on glittery cloth napkins that matched the rich maroon tablecloth.

I looked at my husband, who was eager to help. But I anticipated the danger. "No nibbling the appetizers on the lower refrigerator shelf," I said. "You can have the not-so-pretty ones on the top."

Eager for the perfect day, I didn't sleep much that night.

Christmas morning arrived with the sound of "Jingle Bells" from the radio alarm. I bounced out of bed and ran to put the defrosted, seasoned turkey into the oven. Beside every item on my list, I placed a check mark as soon as it was done. Add torn pieces of dried bread to the crumbled cornbread. Peel the potatoes. Put green and black olives in the crystal serving bowls. Prepare the stuffed celery sticks for the crystal plate.

At the assigned times, I added the broth and placed the dressing below the already cooked turkey. The yams had enough brown sugar to send everyone into a sugar high.

As guests arrived, I calculated where each new food item fit into my meal plan. In the final thirty minutes, I hummed a happy tune. Whipped potatoes steamed from their pan. Toasty brown marshmallows were melting over the yams. Everything was coming together perfectly.

I removed the foil from the roasting pan and slid the turkey back into the oven so it would turn golden brown. As soon as everything was placed, my table would be the ideal picture in Betty Crocker's cookbook. My in-laws were sure to be impressed.

I sighed with a deep feeling of accomplishment

and went to the living room to chat with guests. From across the room, my husband winked at me, as if to say, *Well done*.

Ka-pow! A loud bang from somewhere.

My mother-in-law turned pale. Had she been shot? No, there was no blood.

My husband's eyes widened. "What was *that*?" He jumped out of his recliner.

"Sounded like a gunshot to me." My brother-in-law looked out the street-side window, apparently expecting to see someone dead on the sidewalk.

Nervous laughter and murmurs filled the room.

I stepped toward the dining area and surveyed the candles. Had a votive glass become too hot and burst? No, the sound hadn't come from there.

My husband came toward me. "I think it came from the kitchen."

I rushed to the kitchen with a gaggle of relatives trailing behind. Every dish looked exactly as I'd left it a few minutes earlier. I raised the lid on the stovetop items to take a peek. All was well. Nothing amiss.

I shrugged, my worries fading. "Who knows what it was."

The turkey could use one more basting. Ready for my in-laws to be awed with my culinary skills, I reached for the hot-pads and opened the oven door. Bits and pieces of turkey greeted me—on the inside of the door, the sides of the oven, and in the dressing. The marshmallow-topped yams were dotted with brown meat fragments. The turkey legs hung by thin sinews, and browned skin draped over the edge of the roasting pan.

What had gone wrong? I felt like I'd showed up to work without clothes.

Silence.

Finally, I laughed, more from pain than from joy, and then everyone joined in.

I pulled out the roasting pan and placed it on the stovetop.

My mother-in-law peered at the turkey remains, which looked much like somebody had blasted it with a shotgun at close range. She patted my back and sighed.

I could only respond by shaking my head. My shoulders drooped as I bit my lip. Now, everybody knew my cooking skills were limited. Did it matter? It did to me.

My husband stopped laughing long enough to wipe the tears from his eyes. When he looked at me, he knew it was time to clear the room. He kissed my cheek and returned the electric knife to its box. "Folks, let's head back to the living room and give my wife some space."

As he herded his chuckling clan out of the kitchen, I mouthed to him a grateful *thank you*. Tears filled my eyes as I stared at the ruined meal.

Then I noticed bits of turkey floating in the pan. I popped a piece in my mouth. Wow! This tastes good. I covered the platter with salvaged pieces from the exploded bird, then went to the dining room with the grand announcement: "Time to eat," I said.

We all agreed that the "exploded turkey" tasted as good as well-carved slices, but whenever we have family gatherings, nobody orders my "chef surprise."

Pauper's Tree
by Connie Lewis Leonard

The angel said, "Fear not! For behold I bring you good tidings of great joy." What wonderful words if I could use them to dispel my personal fears. I wanted my son and daughter to enjoy all the wonder and awe of the Christmas miracle, but how was that possible when we had so little?

In 1981, while my husband, Gary, was a second-year student at Southwestern Baptist Seminary, the family lived with only the bare necessities. We had money for only a few gifts—nothing expensive. And we wouldn't have that much if we bought a Christmas tree.

Comfort came from knowing we would be going back "home" to spend an old-fashioned Christmas with my family. Kim and Richie would get to open their gifts on Christmas Eve and Christmas Day by the big, beautifully decorated Christmas tree.

If we had a big tree at our house, the few gifts would look like two acorns under a towering oak. The kids needed to be content with the two-foot green-cellophane tree in storage from our first year of marriage. The tiny artificial tree, with a few little balls and lights, was phony and cheap, reminiscent of the tree in "A Charlie Brown Christmas." It was the best we could do.

While we listened to traditional Christmas music from our long-play phonograph albums, we set out more decorations. We hung our stockings on the mantle of our fake fireplace. The expression on my children's faces revealed their disappointment. Our house lacked the festiveness of Christmases past.

"Let's go driving and look at Christmas lights," I said in an excited tone, thinking the scenery might spark their holiday spirit.

We drove through one of the elite Fort Worth neighborhoods.

Gary and I pointed at the lights and repeated oohs and aahs as we admired the beauty and majesty of the lights reflecting off the lake near the Colonial Country Club. Exquisitely decorated Christmas trees shined from large plate-glass windows and foyers. Endless strings of brilliant color lit up each elaborate estate. Santas and reindeer, snowmen and elves, manger scenes and carolers adorned the yards. The night was aglow with color.

The more Gary and I gushed about the beauty before us, the more quiet the children became. We encouraged them to sing along with the familiar carols playing on the radio, but they weren't in the mood— even though that was our family tradition.

"Is something wrong?" I asked. "You've always enjoyed looking at Christmas lights before."

"We always had a tree before," ten-year-old Kim said, grumbling because she knew we couldn't afford one.

"I wish we weren't poor, so we could have a Christmas tree." Richie was too young to understand why sacrifices were important, but he was old enough to know we didn't have much money.

Richie's sadness sliced through my heart like a scalpel. I wanted him to feel better, but I had already done all I could.

We drove home in silence.

As we pulled onto our street, the DJ on the radio announced a "steal of a deal" at a local lumber store. Since their supply of Christmas trees far outweighed the demand, all their Christmas trees were marked down to the unbelievably low price of three dollars.

Gary and I looked at each other like we had just won a prize. We could afford three dollars.

The children and I went inside, and Gary left in his pickup. While I prepared dinner, Kim and Richie played in the bedroom they shared.

Thirty minutes later, Gary knocked on the door, carrying a nine-foot tightly wrapped Douglas fir tree. "I don't know what it looks like," he said, "but it's tall."

The kids squealed with excitement and tried to pull the tree into the house.

"I'll have to cut it off before we can stand it up," Gary said. "After dinner, we'll decorate it."

After shortening the trunk, Gary brought the tree inside and set it in the stand. He cut the twine, released the tight wrapping, and fluffed out the branches.

When we sat down to dinner, Richie wanted to say the blessing. "Thank you, God, for this food. And thank you, God, for our Christmas tree. And thank you for sending your son, Jesus. Amen."

Proudly, Kim said, "See, Richie. I told you God would answer our prayer."

I didn't understand what Kim was talking about. "What prayer was that?"

Richie giggled. "We asked God for a Christmas tree, and he gave us one."

"You need to understand," Gary said. "We don't always get everything we ask for."

Kim shook her head, as if her faith expected more. "My memory verse last week says, 'All things, whatsoever ye shall ask in prayer, believing, ye shall receive. Matthew 21:22."

"But honey," I said, thinking further explanation was needed, "we can't just ask for everything we want and expect God to give it to us. That verse doesn't mean, every time we want a new dress or a new car, we will get one just because we ask—"

"But we don't need a new car." Kim had always been mature for her age. "Richie is only six years old," she said, "and he *needed* a Christmas tree."

"Ya gotta have faith," Richie said. "I got faith."

After dinner, we unpacked our big strings of Christmas lights and decorations—the special ones that had been gifts, and the precious ones that had been created by our children. The more we decorated the tree, the fluffier it became. This time, as the phonograph record played carols and we admired our tree, the children sang enthusiastically.

The living room was eighteen feet wide by twenty-four feet long, large enough to handle the tall, thin tree. But each day, the branches spread a little. The tree grew fuller and more beautiful. And wider. Gary kept moving the tree farther away from the large picture window until its beauty filled the entire room.

We left the tree up while we went "over the mountains and through the woods" to grandmother's house. A week later, when we returned, the tree had branched out even more—the limbs pressed against the window, still fragrant and alive.

Thanks to the prayers of our children and God's awesome answer, we enjoyed a wonderful Christmas.

Happiness
by Elizabeth Roesch

My sixth-grade teacher said Christmas was the happiest time of the year. How? Was that possible or just wishful thinking? Wherever that feeling came from, I had two more days to find it, or I'd have to wait another year. I might have been only eleven, but I was old enough to know that the magic of Christmas switched off on December 26, as fast as the holiday music vanished from the radio.

"Julie!" Mom's voice. "Downstairs, on the double."

I quickly arranged my stuffed-animal friends. "Stay right here. I'll be back soon." I rushed down the stairs.

Dad's posture at the dining table was enough to tell me something was wrong.

"Get your breakfast." The tension in Mom's voice confirmed what I already sensed. Another fight between Mom and Dad.

My brother took a bite of his toast, saying nothing, never looking up.

This was the silent part. In some ways, I hated the

248

silent part more than the yelling part, which would come in a day or two. The tension made my chest hurt. Where was the Christmas peace and goodwill? I poured milk into my bowl.

"You put the *cereal* in first." Dad's voice cut like a knife.

"You spill milk every time," my brother said. "Why do you keep doing that?"

"I don't know," I said timidly, in hardly more than a whisper. "I just like to."

"Then you like to be stupid."

"That's enough, Billy," Dad said. "I believe I'm the head of this house."

Billy smirked and huffed a short laugh but never took his eyes off his toast. The laugh might have been aimed at Dad, but I was pretty sure he was making fun of me.

I choked down a few bites but couldn't eat any more. Tears slipped down my cheeks as I rinsed my bowl.

"You need to eat more than that, "Mom whispered.

I shook my head and ran upstairs, where I lay on my bed, hugging Panda, my favorite stuffed bear. This time, I felt empty holding him. I sobbed quietly into his chest, not wanting anyone to hear.

When the tears stopped, I put Panda with the other animals.

"This isn't a happy Christmas," I said, expecting the animals to understand. But I knew they didn't.

I tried writing in my diary, but I couldn't explain what the fight was all about. I decided to talk to God instead. "I hate this day, God. If the spirit of Christmas is supposed to bring happiness, I'd like to know how. Dad's mad. Mom's hurt. I hate it when they fight. And they don't care anything about me. I wish you would take me away from here."

To avoid crying again, I needed something to do. I went down the hallway to the craft room, swung open the door, and stopped. Rolls of wrapping paper, ribbon, and bows on the table. The bright Christmas colors and the thought of gifts made me smile. I stepped into the room and touched the foil paper, savoring its elegance.

"Julie!"

Mom's voice snapped me back into reality. She needed me downstairs, and I sure didn't want to get caught snooping. When I spun to leave the room, I saw the stack of gifts half-hidden behind the door. My mind snatched up the image like a flash photo. My presents!

I leaped back into the hallway and leaned against the wall. I pinched my eyes closed, but I couldn't block out the image. It was too late. The surprise of Christmas morning was gone, as quickly and certainly as the flip of a light switch.

I groaned. "Oh, God. Now I've ruined it. What else can go wrong?" If there had been any hope for happiness, it was gone now.

Downstairs, Mom wanted help with baking the cookies. She knew how I loved to scoop the little balls of dough onto the cookie sheet and arrange them in zig-zag rows. This had been a happy time since I was five, but not now. My mind still spun from the shame of discovering my gifts. It was all I could do to finish one tray.

"I'm not feeling good," I said.

Mom touched my forehead. "No fever." She

looked at me like I was faking something. "You'll be fine. You just need to get up and do something. Why don't you put out the nativity set?" Her tone was more a command than a question.

I did what she asked, but there was no happiness in it. I watched the clock, eager for dinner time when my older sister was due to arrive. She had a way of cheering me up, always laughing and playing games with me.

When I helped Mom set the table, I felt a little better. Maybe Mom was right. In staying busy, I might find happiness.

The phone rang. Was it the ring tone or the timing of the call that made me sad?

"Oh, I'm so sorry," Mom said. "We'll miss you."

I already had the message. Mom didn't have to tell me. My sister wasn't coming after all. I didn't ask why. I didn't cry, although I wanted to. I wondered if it was possible to use up all my tears in one day, so I couldn't cry anymore. What was wrong with me? Maybe looking for happiness wasn't a good thing.

After dinner, I slipped my coat over my shoulders like a cape and sat on the back porch steps. Beyond the trees, the lights of downtown shined brightly. Only a few stars twinkled, one of them much brighter than the others, probably a planet. The air was rapidly getting colder. I put my arms through the coat sleeves, dropped the hood over my head, and pulled the zipper. Snuggled into the warmth, I let myself relax.

I sighed deeply, leaned back, and soaked in the beauty of the night sky. In an instant, I sensed that God was close by. He'd been there all along, but I hadn't noticed his presence, not really. He hadn't spoken

251

anything to my heart. He was just there, sitting silently by my side.

As I focused on him, I sensed a knowing look in his eyes. He understood me. He loved me. He felt the pain in my heart, the loneliness—as if it were his own.

I looked toward the stars, more numerous now, and brighter. "Oh, my! God, look how big the universe is." In the depths beyond, billions more stars lay beyond what I could see. "God, you've got to be even bigger than all this, because you created everything. But here you are, sitting right beside me." A chill went up my spine, and I pulled my coat tighter. "I know you have more important things to do. Thank you for being here and for being my friend."

As the darkness deepened and the stars brightened even more, I imagined the largest star shining above Bethlehem. The wise men had a long, hard journey. They followed that star and found the king. So had I.

Joy flooded my heart and wet my cheeks with tears. Finally, I had found it.

Happiness.

Wrapping Up
by Henry McLaughlin

"What a beautiful day," my wife said.

I cringed when I heard her words. A fresh six-inch blanket of snow had fallen on our little community as if dumped by the world's largest Tonka truck. I didn't have to look out the window to see the icicles hanging from the rooftops, glistening like diamond pendants. I could feel the cold air stinging my cheeks. In an unconscious reaction, I squinted from the bright sun reflecting off the snow.

"I think I'll stay home and catch up on stuff," I said, reading the subtext behind her admiration of the landscape. She wanted me to go Christmas shopping with her. I wanted to stay home and relax.

Even if I wasn't leaving, I had to make it possible for others to go. I also had to appear industrious, or I might be deprived of leaning back in my easy chair to read a book. When peace and quiet has been earned, it's even more enjoyable. In the next thirty minutes, I shoveled the snow from the walk to the driveway, edge-to-edge, door to street.

Our kids had completed their snow sculpting. Snow forts bordered the driveway and the street, connected by a labyrinth of tunnels. Supplies of snowballs were cached away, ready to withstand any assaults. Snowmen stood as rotund sentries, watching with their eyes of coal but never speaking. Snow angels invoked divine protection.

Christmas was only a few days away, and I was working my annual shopping plan: let my wife do it. I waved to her and my daughter Meaghan as they left. The three boys continued their winter-long street hockey game at their friend's house. Our eldest daughter Shannon was diligently pursuing her college studies at the nearby campus library.

The house belonged to me. I was ready to get busy. Even the cat got out of my way, running to the girl's bedroom where she loved to curl up on the bed.

It was time to plunge deep into my recliner with my new book. Halfway through chapter two, I put the book down. This wasn't working. What should I be doing? When my wife got home, would she think I had wasted the day? From somewhere, the idea struck me: *I could help her by wrapping Christmas presents.* I resisted, saying, *Get thee behind me, Satan.* I picked up the book and let a few more pages drift before my eyes. I only saw the words. I didn't grasp the meaning, because my mind was occupied with the work I needed to do. I closed the book and shut my eyes. *This too shall pass.*

I popped an old movie into the VCR and lay on the couch, hoping the idea would dissipate in the drama of *The Maltese Falcon.* It didn't.

Where were the wrapping supplies? If my wife hadn't bought them yet, that would be a sign that my need to work had come from an eggnog hangover. Nope. I found everything I needed in the bedroom closet—rolls of Christmas paper, tape, and scissors. The ribbons and bows and name tags were on the top shelf. I was down to one remaining excuse. Where were the presents that needed to be wrapped?

The whole family knew that answer. There are only so many places where Mom could hide presents. I admired my kids for never sneaking up to the attic to take a peak. Or were they so good with their sneaking that I never knew? If so, the presents still needed to be wrapped so they could act surprised.

I had everything I needed. No excuses. I got myself organized, putting my top priorities first: a cup of tea followed by lunch. Then I needed to finish watching that movie. The unwrapped presents still begged for attention. Time to go to work.

Two hours later, I was sitting in the middle of the living room with scraps of wrapping paper littering the floor. Here and there, scrunched-up wads of paper that had been cut too small dotted the carpet like rainbow-colored bocce balls.

A few neatly wrapped presents sat under the tree.

Other unwrapped gifts awaited my creative expressions. I spilled the package of bows while reaching for the tape dispenser. I expected to find it with the rolls of wrapping paper, but it had made its usual journey to hide behind my back at the moment I needed it. The scissors were again burrowed under the paper. I had never before met inanimate objects so adept at playing hide-and-seek. It was the cat's fault.

Princess was strutting about like she was the queen, as if the purpose of humans was to simply feed and amuse her. She decided to share in the spirit of Christmas by leaping onto the presents, sprawling on the spread-out paper, and testing the thickness of the wrapping with her claws. She attacked the tape dispenser like it was the greatest threat to catkind since the creation of the dog. She was as useful to me as snow skis at the beach.

"Go back to bed," I said, as if I thought she would listen. The temptation to trim her whiskers percolated along with those words of wisdom: *It's always easier to get forgiveness than permission.* However, she didn't stay still long enough for me to enact my plot. Exasperated, I stuck a big red bow on her head.

Princess looked at me with great disdain, as if she had been crowned with something other than gold. She pranced away, trying to shake off the offensive chapeau without losing her dignity.

Only minutes after Princess left, I heard the back door open and close.

"Hey, Dad! I'm home." Shannon's tone came as a warning, as if any secrets should be concealed before she came in.

I glanced to my side, making sure her presents were snuggled under the tree. Yes, there they were, in their shiny multi-colored paper. "I'm in here," I said.

She walked into the living room and surveyed the scene with the air that only a college sophomore can present. She pointed at the tree. "Dad, did you wrap all those presents?" She seemed startled at the wondrous sight of my endeavors.

"Yes, I did."

"That's pretty good." She paused. "Because usually, white men can't wrap." She maintained a perfectly deadpan expression.

I sat for a moment, silenced and dumfounded, as the victim of a budding comic genius. "That's a good one, Shannon. I'm proud of you."

As she walked into the kitchen, she said with shock and dismay, "Oh, my goodness. I've turned into my father."

Big Plans
by Marie Loper Maxwell

After endless blood tests and using fertility drugs
that didn't seem to help, my husband, Sean, and I celebrated when I became pregnant. Then we grieved when
I miscarried. Later, pregnant again, I had fresh hope
until I miscarried for the second time. I desperately
wanted a child, but understood from experience—
children were a gift from God. I wasn't doing well on
my own.

On March 30, 2010, my son Jackson Joseph was
born, an answer to countless prayers. A miracle, considering my battle with infertility and miscarriages. Jackson was absolutely perfect: ten-and-a-half pounds,
twenty-two inches long, with innocent, dark blue eyes
that melted my heart.

Three days before Thanksgiving, just eight months
after wrapping Jackson in a blanket and bringing him
home from the hospital, I found out I was pregnant
again. This was good news. Or was it? I worried that I
might miscarry again but thanked God for his gift.

I was so excited, but for a while I didn't want to

tell Sean. He was a widower with two daughters. This baby would make four children in our family. What would this do to our finances? Sean was already working seven days a week. We were still recovering from the cost of my maternity leave with Jackson. Would he be as excited as I was?

"This is strange timing," I said, stammering. "Kind of unbelievable, Sean. I'm pregnant!"

First, a look of disbelief, then surprise and extreme pleasure. "That's wonderful. Babies are blessings. When will new baby Maxwell get here?"

"I think it will be the end of July."

Sean gave me a big hug. "God has great things in store for us."

With his arms wrapped around me, I felt secure, comforted, and confident that this pregnancy could not fail. Relieved, I went back to my housework and caring for little Jackson.

As a teacher, I looked forward to this Christmas as much as most people, maybe more. Two whole weeks off work. Jackson's first Christmas. Time at my parents' house. And rest—oh, how my pregnant body cried for rest.

When we arrived at my parents' house, Mom picked up Jackson and whispered in his ear. "Jackson, you're going to love your first Christmas."

"Oh, Jackson," his sisters said in an excited tone, "we get to open presents soon."

"Look, Jackson," my father said. "That gift has your name on it."

I couldn't wait to see Jackson unwrap his gifts. He was sure to love his first Christmas.

The next few days were filled with laughter, love,

and food.

Jackson loved the walker my parents had waiting for him. He could pick up great speed on the stained concrete floors. "Pawpaw," he screamed as he looked for my father.

On Christmas Eve, Sean and his mom arrived.

We put the giddy girls down for the night and finished wrapping gifts. Finally, Jackson was out for the night, and I could get a few hours' sleep before the Christmas morning festivities. I dressed for bed and made a restroom stop, hoping I wouldn't have to get up too many times during the night.

Oh, no! The one thing a pregnant woman never wants to see. My heart sank. Although I had heard about women bleeding and still having a successful pregnancy, I knew what was happening. Both my previous miscarriages began with the same little spots of blood.

"Oh, God," I said, my anger building. "Why is this happening again?" And why now, during our Christmas celebration? I desperately wanted a miracle—to somehow have this baby. "Dear God," I said, "You created this life inside of me. You have plans for this baby— great plans—to further your Kingdom." I tried to think of an argument why God would have to listen to me. "I pray *blessings* for this baby, Lord. I pray *protection* for this sweet baby. You love this baby even more than I do, Lord. Please, God, protect this baby's life."

I walked to the bedroom, lay down beside Sean, and silently wept myself to sleep.

The next morning, I decided not to share my news. "I didn't sleep well last night," I said, making excuse for the sadness on my face.

Following our family tradition, the girls told the Christmas story. We prayed and thanked God for his son and opened our gifts. Sleepy-eyed, Jackson wasn't sure what the excitement was all about. We all laughed when he chose to play with the wrapping paper and bows while ignoring the gifts inside. The family was having a great time.

I managed to smile, only tearing up twice. I hoped everybody would think my emotion came from seeing Jackson's first Christmas. Actually, I was silently praying for my unborn baby. *Lord, please sustain this baby's life.*

On my next trip to the restroom, there was no bleeding, but I felt more cramping. Finally, I had to tell Mom and my sister what was happening.

Mom understood, having had two miscarriages herself. She knew what it was like to cherish the life inside of you and despair when that life was lost.

They prayed with me and cried with me. "God will protect your baby," they said in faith believing. Mom phoned my aunt, and she began to pray. We described our need to the prayer chain at church. I texted my prayer-warrior friends.

I wasn't feeling any better, but I wasn't feeling any worse either. I phoned the doctor, wanting to hear good news but fearing the worst.

"Come in on Monday," the doctor said. "In the meantime, lie down and try to relax, in a position that will help the cramping to stop."

For three days I lay there, missing much of the festivities, my mood often shifting from hope for a miracle to anger over the loss. My mom kept telling me she had faith that our baby would arrive in July, just as planned. I wanted to have faith, but it was so hard when the evidence pointed in the opposite direction.

On Monday morning, I was the first patient to arrive at the obstetrician's office. I sat with Sean in the waiting room, praying, trying to believe I would see the tiny heartbeat I so desperately wanted.

We were ushered back to the sonogram room.

Dr. Emmet walked in. "I hear your Christmas was rough," she said.

I nodded and started crying.

"Well let's take a look." She squirted goo on my belly and slowly rolled the device back and forth.

I held my breath, trying to concentrate on the screen.

"There it is. Can you see it?" she asked.

A heartbeat. I cried even harder, this time in overflowing gratitude. All I could say was, "Thank you, God!"

On July 22, my Christmas prayer was answered. Carter Randy Maxwell was born. Ten pounds, one ounce. Twenty-and-a-half inches long.

As I wrapped the blanket around my baby to take him home from the hospital, I whispered in his ear. "God has big plans for you."

Stocking Thief
by Olivia Womack

When Mom and I went shopping, I saw what I wanted at the toy store. There she was, a gorgeous beauty standing on the shelf by herself—the perfect gift for any girl—a doll with red hair and freckles, just like me. Her yellow dress was trimmed in blue, with a matching slip. I cuddled her in my arms. Her tiny golden slippers brought my wishful sigh. She was lovely. Best of all, when I squeezed her tummy, she giggled a delightful laugh. Instinctively, I giggled each time I heard her. After that, I felt sad because I had to put her back. She cost more than my parents could afford.

I dreamed about finding my doll under the Christmas tree. I named her Rosie for her red hair, rosy cheeks, and sunny personality. I also had nightmares when I saw myself searching, but she wasn't there. What could I do? My six-year-old mind went to work, putting a plan together. When Santa came on Christmas Eve, his sleigh would be filled with toys, including my doll. All I had to do was catch him while he was leaving toys and tell him I wanted Rosie.

263

Late on Christmas Eve, the smell from cinnamon candles and fresh-baked sugar cookies reminded me that Santa would be coming soon. The blinking lights on the Christmas tree flashed their soft rainbow colors. I'd been on my best behavior for months and deserved the number-one gift on my Santa list.

With my pajama sleeve, I rubbed a circle on the frosted window and peered up into the darkness. Santa and his reindeer had to be out there somewhere, soaring across the sky, but I couldn't even see the stars. I could hardly wait for him to arrive. How late would it be? Whenever it was, he wouldn't come unless I was in bed, appearing to be asleep.

Our family tradition included filling a stocking with fruit, pecans, and small gifts for each family member. I'd saved my allowance for several weeks to buy Mom a silver bracelet and Dad a box of chocolate covered cherries. I placed the treasures inside their stockings and peeked inside mine. Empty. Disappointed, I laid my stocking on the fireplace hearth and hurried to the kitchen to fix Santa a plate of goodies.

Decorative sugar cookies, fudge, and hot cocoa would keep Santa from flying back up the chimney. His hungry tummy would bring the delay I needed to catch him and tell him what I wanted. I set the tasty treats next to my stocking.

"The sooner you fall asleep, the sooner Christmas Day will come," Mom said.

I kissed Mom and Dad goodnight and jumped into bed, but I needed to stay awake. I thought about how much fun Rosie and I would have together. We would be pretend beauty queens, dancing like Cinderella at the ball, our long white dresses swishing across the floor.

Instead of a carriage, we could ride in a convertible with the top down, letting our red hair flow with the breeze. An endless list of ideas tumbled through my mind. With each new picture, my dreams became more real. I snuggled under the bedcovers and closed my eyes.

Bang! Where was I? A cold wind whistled outside my window. Snowflakes splattered the window pane, collecting on the sill. Whop! Bang!

I sat up in bed. "It's Santa!" I whispered. "He's here."

The loud thumps sounded as if our chimney had been too small, trapping Santa until he came crashing to the floor. In a dash, I tiptoed to the living room to catch him before he finished his cookies. I peeked around the doorway.

"Get him," Mom yelled, bouncing up and down on the sofa. "There he is. Get him!"

Dad whapped the broom against the floor. He struck so hard, the breeze flapped his red polka-dot boxer shorts around his hairy bowlegs.

Why are they beating up Santa? He'll never come now. Not tonight. Not ever!

Dad flailed the broom from high over his head, brushing the living room ceiling. "I'll get him. Look out!" The broom thundered when it slammed against the hardwood floor.

When I stepped into the living room, a gray critter skittered across my foot, pushing a pecan in front of its nose. A mouse! I jumped onto the coffee table, not sure where the monster had gone. Then I jumped onto the sofa with Mom. The sofa became a trampoline as Mom and I bounced up and down.

Again Dad struck the floor at the intruder. With

each blow of the broom, Mom screamed new instructions and shooed it with her gown.

In mid-bounce, I glanced toward the Christmas tree and saw the yellow dress with blue trim. I squealed. "My wish came true. Santa brought Rosie!" The cookie plate was empty. Santa had already come. The Christmas tree lights blinked off and on, flashing a multicolored halo around her head. Now I had a new emergency to worry about. "Look out, Dad. Don't hit Rosie."

The mouse pushed his pecan toward the tree, acting more like a squirrel than a mouse.

"I've got you now," Dad said, striking at the tree.

The branches swayed to the left, then to the right, causing the bells to jingle and ornaments to fall off. The blinking lights went out.

I lunged. "Rosie! I'll save you." I snatched up Rosie seconds before the tree came crashing to the floor.

Rosie and I lay hidden among the pine branches, tangled in tinsel. Rosie giggled in my ear. Where was the mouse? In my other ear, I heard a tiny squeal and scampering through the branches. I jerked away, wanting to escape both the mouse and the next strike of the broom.

I thought, *Look out, mouse. You're in big trouble now. Dad's gonna get you.*

"Quick," Mom said, "open the door."

Dad leaped to obey.

The mouse darted for the opening, still rolling that pecan in front of his nose. With Mom and Dad looking over our shoulders, Rosie and I watched the mouse burrow into the wet snow with his pecan. He had his treasure, and I had mine.

The house was a mess, but we laughed until our sides ached.

When I became a parent, I often reminded my kids of that true Christmas Eve story. Now, I tell my grandchildren about the stocking thief who refused to let go of his Christmas gift.

When the family is snuggled in their beds, I hang stockings by the fireplace, filled with fruit, pecans, and small gifts. If I drop a pecan and it rolls across the floor, I hear echoes of laughter from long ago when one of God's little creatures caused a ruckus, made a mess, and brought laughs that helped knit our family together.

I'll always be thankful for my encounter with the stocking thief.

Hurry Up and Wait
by Shari Pouncey

Unable to bear the thought of disappointing my granddaughters, I watched the clock at work like a traffic light, waiting for it to tell me I could go. On Christmas Eve, other bosses would have let me leave early, but my boss demanded a full day's work before and after a holiday. Keeping me there wasn't helping him. My mind wasn't on my work.

Draped in tinsel and silver bells, even the clock was part of the festive office décor. Every evening I passed the twelve-foot Christmas tree in the lobby, decked out in twinkling lights, gold bows, and personalized ornaments. The Christmas songs playing over the speakers reminded me that I was running out of time. I still didn't have the Barbie dolls that Amiya and Andrea wanted for Christmas. Today was my last chance.

The moment the second hand clicked to 4:59:59, I raced out the doors and into the breath-snatching cold December wind, determined to be first one out of the parking lot. Nothing, not even the harshness of nature, could keep me from getting to that blue-light special where I would buy the cute Barbies for my babies.

If the Barbies hadn't been so popular, the stores wouldn't have been sold out every time I tried to buy them. Fortunately, one store had a new shipment and was having a special sale to bring in last-minute shoppers. The sale started at 6:00 p.m., and their entire stock would be gone in a few minutes. As I headed down the Interstate, I wondered if I could make it in time. On Christmas Eve, I expected the rush-hour traffic to be light, but it wasn't.

I glanced at the rearview mirror. A tan Cadillac with a wreath on the front was approaching at a ridiculous speed. He swerved into the narrow space in front of me, about the length of a parallel parking space. His tires squealed and mine did too, as I hit my horn to keep from slamming into him. I got a close look at his bumper and the sticker that said: *If you are a Christian, honk twice.*

Was he trying to make me a Christian or take away my salvation? As if he could hear me, I yelled, "I did honk twice, Mister—in self-defense." If I hadn't been shaking, I would have laughed.

The man rolled down his window, pointed his finger toward the sky, and yelled something. I believe he was sending me a message, and not an inspirational one.

I thought, *If you had been patient, I would have gladly let you into my lane. You didn't have to be nasty about it.* Patience is a lost art for so many people these days, but maybe I could sympathize. I was in a hurry too.

At the department store, I rushed past the people standing around the store entrance, ignoring whatever they might be waiting for. I knew where I needed to be

269

and was determined to get there—to the spot nearest to the toy department. I was ready for a mad sprint to the blue-light display as soon as the guards would let us go.

The blue lights flashed, and the crowd took off like the start of a fifty-meter dash. My athletic training came in handy. I was thankful for other items on special so the entire throng wasn't coming my way. Even so, I arrived amid a packed group with a thousand hands reaching for the shelves. I grabbed one Barbie from the shelf and another right out of the reaching hands of a shopper who looked like she might be trying to make a decision. "That's not your color," I said.

I weaved my way through packed aisles, gathered several other gift items, and hurried to check out. The carts were bunched up at the registers like bumper-to-bumper freeway traffic during rush hour, crawling along as if maneuvering slick roads in an ice storm.

My feet throbbed from the long day, hectic shopping, and prolonged standing. I focused on the lines around me and dashed to get into the shorter one. As soon as I moved, eager to go forward quickly, my line slowed while my previous line moved ahead of me. What was wrong with these people that they couldn't just pay for the merchandise and go? This was not a time to visit with the cashier or go check on something. They should know if their credit cards were maxed out, shouldn't they? I bit my lip to keep my mouth shut.

Fuming and disappointed, I headed to the jewelry checkout register, only to find that department with a long line too. There was no sense in going back to the other long lines and starting over. I decided to stay.

A voice sounded over the loud speaker. "Ladies and gentleman, I am Mrs. Olivia Winn." The voice and the name were familiar. I assumed she was some kind of celebrity because the place exploded with screams of excitement. Both the young and old were dancing and yelling like children, as if they knew something good was coming.

"Ladies and gentleman," Mrs. Winn said, "I'm happy to announce, because of your patience at the store today, everyone who is currently standing in lines one through thirteen will receive a three-hundred-dollar gift certificate.

Another round of high-pitched squeals of excitement echoed throughout the building, reminding me of frantic roller-coaster riders.

I turned to the woman standing behind me. "Who did the announcer say she was?"

"Oh, she's Olivia Winn, the television host." The woman had a surprised, patronizing look, as if nobody should ever need to ask such a silly question.

Then I remembered the outrageously popular *Olivia Winn Reality Show*. I should have known. I was stunned, realizing what I had missed because of my impatience. I wanted my old place in line, but people would think I was trying to cheat my way to the prize. They would be right. By switching lines, I was trying to get ahead. Not only had I failed to get out of the store any faster, I had cheated myself out of a prize. Wasn't that what the Bible said—that I need patience to receive the promise?

I drove out of the parking lot thinking about how many of God's blessings I might have missed because I was in such a hurry. Then I thought about the Barbie dolls that needed to be wrapped before I could go to my granddaughters' house to celebrate Christmas. I was supposed to be there by eight o'clock, but I had lost a lot of time at the store. What would they think if I was late?

I needed to hurry.

Christmas Dollar
by Wayne Johnson

Christmas vacation was only two weeks away. I wished my teacher hadn't made us draw names for the school party. My dad had a good job, but I was afraid to ask him for money to buy Julie a gift. What was I going to do? Each day, I became more worried. I was running out of time.

Three days before the party, I was walking to my third-grade class at Crossland Elementary. When I cut across the parking area at the Shell station on Carrollton Avenue, I couldn't believe my eyes. An old and dirty dollar bill lay flat on the pavement, rumpled like it had been run over by a few cars leaving the gas station.

In 1959, a dollar was a lot of money. It would buy four gallons of gas, five loaves of bread, or twenty-five first-class postage stamps. I neatly folded the bill in thirds and placed it in the right front pocket of my jeans. I'm thinking, *This is my lucky day.*

All day at school, I thought about what I would buy. In almost every class, I pulled out the bill for another look. Yes, it was real—dirty, wrinkled, and

273

perforated, but definitely still worth a dollar. Each time, I carefully folded it and tucked it into my front pocket.

When the last bell rang, I rushed past my class-mates and sprinted down Carrollton Avenue. At home, I threw open the door and jumped up and down while waving my dollar bill. "Look, Mom. L-look what I found. I found a w-whole dollar." I paused to catch my breath. "N-now I can b-buy a Christmas gift for Julie."

Mom didn't show the excitement I expected. "Where did you find it?"

"Just l-lying there—on the pavement down at the S-shell station on the c-corner." So far, my explanation didn't seem to be sufficient. "This m-morning, I was cutting across the parking lot and there it was—l-lying there—f-flat as a pancake. I picked it up and put it in my pocket for s-safe keeping." I held the dollar high and waved it. "I've never f-found something like this before. This is my l-lucky day."

"Did you ask the people at the station if they had lost a dollar bill?" Mom wasn't smiling. "Did you go into the little building where the attendants sit when they aren't pumping gas? Did you ask any of them if they lost a dollar bill?"

"N-no."

"Why not?"

"Uh… it was just l-lying on the pavement. No one was around, so I p-picked it up." I stared at the floor, not feeling excited anymore. "It w-wasn't even near the place w-where the men s-stay."

"Well, you need to ask them if they lost a dollar. If they did, you must give it back."

"B-but it's mine. I f-found it."

"If they lost the money, they deserve to have it

back, right?"

"B-but why, Mom? I f-found it."

"Wayne, listen to me. Ask the men if anyone lost a dollar bill. If someone says he lost it, you must give it back. You can keep the dollar if no one claims it. That's fair, isn't it?"

"But I f-found it, fair and s-square."

"Think of it this way: if you lost a dollar and someone found it, wouldn't you want that person to give it back?"

I stared at the dollar. The dirt and the wrinkles didn't lessen the value of what I held in my hand.

"Well?" Mom said. "Wouldn't you want him to give it back?"

"Yes, Ma'am." Every part of my being rebelled against the thought of facing those men. "But I don't w-want to go in there. They will l-laugh at me when I don't s-say my words right. Please don't m-make me go."

"Honey, if you want to keep the dollar, you have to ask them. If you don't go, you can't keep the money. I'll give it to whoever says he lost it."

My hand trembled, and I was about to cry.

"I tell you what," she said. "I'll go with you. We can leave a few minutes early for school. If no one claims the dollar, you can keep it. Otherwise, you can't. What do you want to do?"

"Okay, I'll go." I said the words, but I would rather have fought a fire-breathing dragon than face those men. I wished I had never shown Mom what I found. At least I'd still have my dollar. This way, I could both lose the dollar and be ridiculed.

The next morning, I begged and pleaded, but Mom

275

wouldn't budge. At the gas station, I pointed out the exact spot on the pavement where I found the dollar, in a last-ditch effort to avoid the men. It didn't work.

No cars were at the gas station, so all the men were inside when we arrived at the door. I waited for Mom to enter, but she put me in the lead. The man farthest away reached up and turned off the radio. The old "swamp cooler" air conditioner churned with the pounding of my heart as a lump rose in my throat. All three men wore brown service station uniforms with a yellow Shell logo above the shirt pocket.

The man with grease on his shirt looked at Mom. "Yes, Ma'am. Can I help you?"

I felt a hand in the middle of my back, pushing me forward, followed by a whisper. "Go on. Ask them."

I pulled the dollar from my pocket and held it up between my first finger and thumb. "Yesterday on m-my w-w-way to s-school, I f-found… I f-found… I found this dollar in your parking lot?" Words had never been harder to push out of my mouth. I felt like a big bully was sitting on my chest, taking away all my breath. "Did anybody l-lose a dollar?" My mouth was as dry as West Texas cotton, and the dollar waved because my hand was trembling.

The words were out, but the pressure wasn't gone. I braced myself for the teasing. "On your w-w-way to school?" one man would ask. Another man would say, "Y-y-yeah. I l-lost a d-dollar y-yesterday." Then they would all laugh, and I would have to be strong and not cry. I waited for their fun to begin.

The older man turned to the others. "Did you boys lose a dollar bill?"

The man by the radio checked his wallet. "Not me.

All my dollars are right here."

The third man shook his head. "I didn't. And I haven't heard of anybody else who lost any money."

"Well," the first man said with a smile, "I haven't lost a dollar either. Looks like you have just found yourself a dollar."

My wobbling knees became steady. Now the dollar was mine, and no one had made fun of my stuttering. I folded the bill and slipped it into my pocket. It felt so good to do what I knew was right. "Thank you," I said to the men.

I should have said "thank you" to Mom. Her insistence that I go was the best Christmas gift she could have given me.

First Christmas Recipe
by Carol Hatheway Scott

1	**dirty stable (do not substitute inn.)**
	assorted smelly barn animals
1	**anxious husband**
1	**mother ripe with child**
	swaddling clothes
1	**manger, well used**
1	**field of shepherds**
	light from the glory of the Lord
1	**sky full of angels**

Mix first four ingredients in Bethlehem until well blended. Allow mother to give birth.

Carefully fold baby into swaddling clothes and lay in manger.

Terrify shepherds by lighting the night skies with the Lord's Glory. Add one angel announcing the birth of the Savior. Let shepherds chill. Add remaining angels. Allow their praises to rise above the fields. Compel shepherds to find baby and spread news of

278

Savior's birth throughout Bethlehem. Marinate ingredients while mother ponders everything.

Serve generous portions often.

Expect 180° turns.

Seasonal. Recipe first appeared in the Bible, Luke 2.

Christmas Restored
by Melanie Wallace

It's Christmas morning! I awakened with eager anticipation, trying to imagine all the things I would get. Still dark. A little chilly, the best I could hope for on the Texas coast. Never any snow. It was too early to get up, so I lay in bed, daydreaming of countless surprises.

I already knew what my little sister, Annie, was getting. I helped put her gifts together, then wrapped them and put them under the tree. I had no idea about Lynette, my older sister. And me? I could only guess. Would I get that pair of wedge sandals I wanted? Whatever I got, it had to be as much as my sisters got. That was only fair.

An eternity passed before I heard someone else awake. I rolled out of bed and raced to the living room, where the Christmas tree welcomed me with its glorious colored lights and sequined balls. There they were—all the gifts—wrapped in flashy red and gold, with fancy bows. The pile had grown overnight, and that meant a bunch of goodies for me.

My little sister ran to play with her unwrapped

gifts, her baby doll and stroller. Dad and Mom called out the names on the wrapped packages.

Christmas paper went flying. Bows going here, boxes stacked there. I unwrapped one package after another. I had plenty to brag about, including the perfect pair of bronze-colored wedge sandals—everything an eleven-year-old girl could want. Done with unwrapping and admiring my treasures, I wondered what my older sister had gotten.

Lynette was still unwrapping presents, which wasn't fair. If we had received the same number, we should have finished at the same time. A picture for the wall. A cute little lamp. What would she do with all that stuff? She wanted to redecorate her room, but did she really need all this?

I slumped against the couch, confirming what I already knew. My parents loved her more than me. Lynette was the oldest. The pet. The one who always made Dad proud. Why not me? She was only a year-and-a-half older.

Annie was Mom and Dad's baby girl.

I was caught in the middle—unloved, unappreciated, and seldom noticed. It just wasn't fair. The more I thought about the injustice, the more angry I became, like a volcano building pressure, ready to erupt. When the hot lava burned my tongue, I couldn't keep quiet.

"It isn't fair," I said. "Lynette has a lot more than me." I had to stake my claim—take what I was due. "You should give me one of her presents."

"What are you talking about?" Dad looked offended. "You got as much as your sister—almost to the penny."

I feasted my eyes on all the loot my sister had

gained. "No I didn't. She's got more." I didn't know whether to stomp my feet or cry. I felt like doing both.

Dad and Mom tried to console me.

I wasn't buying it. I wanted what had to be Lynette's prized possession—all in the interest of fairness. I pointed at the framed picture. "Those flowers match *my* furniture, not hers. It belongs in my room."

Lynette didn't look happy, but she didn't protest when I took the picture and put it on my stack of gifts.

Dad and Mom didn't say anything, evidently waiting for the problem to solve itself.

Later that day, I hung the picture on my wall, feeling justified. Now we were even.

Every day, I passed that picture. I tried not to notice, because it reminded me how gracious my sister had been and how I was a thief. It belonged to her, but I had taken it.

When I grew older and moved to my own place, that picture didn't fit. Or maybe it did, but I didn't want it to fit. I needed to forget the past so I could ignore my guilt. I was doing just fine, raising a family, feeling good about myself, until one day, my younger sister said something about our rooms when we were kids. I felt like I was standing before a judge, convicted again.

I didn't have the picture anymore, yet its presence still haunted me. What could I do?

A soft, tender voice spoke to my heart. *Return your sister's present. This must be reconciled—for your benefit—and for hers.*

I got the message. Lynette had to be restored with what was hers by right, and I needed to right a wrong, no matter how many years had passed.

I went to one store after another, not sure what

would replace the picture I no longer had. Nothing grabbed me. Framed quotes—poems—pictures with flowers—but nothing spoke from my heart.

With a blank canvas and some of my son's paints, I began my adventure to let Lynette know that neither God nor I had not forgotten her. She was loved, and we both wanted to restore what had been taken from her.

The paint had barely dried when I gathered my family for the three-hour trip to my sister's house. I could have sent the painting by mail with a letter, but that wasn't good enough. With everyone snuggled on the couches or seated on chairs, I told my story, admitted my guilt, and made amends.

My restoration made this a Christmas to remember—one that I would never want to forget.

Making a Scene
by Rhodema Cargill

Silent night, quiet night, and all was calm. Now was the time for Mom to get the Christmas decorating done, which she couldn't do during the day.

My four children, already in bed, dreamed of dancing sugar plums or squirming gummy-worms. My husband, after a hard weekend of physician calls at the hospital, was already down for his long winter's nap. The evening was mine. Time to decorate.

With a huge carton of decorations in my arms, balanced in front of me, I stepped silently down the stairs, hoping I wouldn't cause one of my household creatures to stir. Unable to see over or around the box, I extended my foot until it reached the next step. Easy there. Unable to use the handrail, I had to be careful lest I lose my balance and take a tumble.

Halfway down, I turned around so I could see the steps. Much better, although I still had to be careful. I finally made it to the level floor of the entryway and took a deep breath. I rested the box on the small table in the library, where we homeschooled.

"Ahh… Eee…! A scream out of nowhere, followed by the blond head of my seven-year-old Ryan, popping up behind the box. "Did I scare you?" He looked as happy as Christmas morning, sure he had scared me half out of my wits.

He had. If he had been an angel, the appropriate announcement would have been, "Fear not!"

"Son, what are you doing out of bed?"

Clad in his fireman pajamas, his hair slicked down after his bath, Ryan hopped from one foot to the other, as if he were stepping on hot coals. He stopped to give me a serious look. "I thought we needed to pray."

Again? Was this an excuse to stay up? He had way too much energy.

He looked at the box on the table. "Hey! How will I do school tomorrow with this big box on my desk?"

His three older sisters were easy to handle, but Ryan? Frustrating. His sweet toddler and preschool disposition had transformed into an uncontrollable monster—full steam ahead without caution. Patience was no longer a virtue within his grasp. Bedtime was always a battleground. He could not turn off the energy, quiet his mind, and drift off to sleep. His oldest sister asked if I fed him rocket fuel for breakfast. His actions suggested I might be doing that for lunch and dinner as well.

Ryan had talent. He was smart, and he seemed to know it. He could create a crisis that pulled my attention away from his misbehavior. Instead of commanding him to get back to bed, I found myself explaining why the box was there.

"It's the Baby Jesus nativity set that I set up each year for you kids. As soon as I get the Christmas

285

decorations put out, the table will be clear. We will have school tomorrow, same as usual."

Standing on tiptoe, Ryan peered into the box, checking out the mismatched crumples of holiday tissue paper that protected every piece of the set.

An idea came to mind, a way to avoid a battle. "Ryan, would you like to help set up the nativity set?" My kind offer was followed by a command. "After that, you *will* go to bed."

With a look of shock and wide-eyed delight, he tore into the box without saying a word, unwrapping each piece as if he were in a timed race. He flung the paper like someone looking for treasure.

Un-crumpled pieces sailed past me like paper airplanes. "Hey! Watch it, Ryan. Please! Be more careful."

He was flying, and he wasn't in the mood to land. Thankfully, the pieces weren't breakable. Or were they? I didn't want to find out.

The traditional shelf at the kids' eye level was already cleared and ready.

Ryan started to put the pieces in their appropriate places. He found the stable in the bottom of the box. "Here it is," he shouted, loud enough that I wondered if he would wake up everyone else in the house. He placed it on the center of the shelf. Baby Jesus went in the middle, between Mary and Joseph. Next, he turned his attention to the animals.

How cute. Since he needed no coaching, I stepped back and watched, thankful he would soon be going to bed.

No, wait. What was he doing? "Is that where the sheep belong?" I asked, hoping he'd understand that all the animals didn't belong *inside* the stable. There wasn't room.

Apparently not hearing me, Ryan kept adding pieces inside the stable.

I shook my head. Everybody knew the wise men should be approaching from *outside* the stable, on the right, coming from the east. The shepherds belonged outside on the left, waiting for their turn to see the baby.

Obviously, Ryan had a different idea. He barely had room to squeeze in the little drummer boy.

"Son," I said, unable to control myself any longer, "don't you think it's a little crowded in the stable?"

No answer.

His work finished, Ryan stepped back with a look of satisfaction, holding both hands wide as if to explain the obvious. "Mom, they didn't come all that way to stand around in the yard. They all want to be inside with Baby Jesus because they love him."

What could I say? I had no words to offer in response. He was right.

My harried heart was stilled, and starry lights mingled with my tears. My son had taught me an important lesson, which called for a time of prayer before I sent him to bed.

Ryan prayed for Grampa's knee, our dogs, and what he wanted for Christmas. I thanked God for the wisdom I had received from my energetic son.

We joined those in the crowded stable, gazed into the face of Jesus, making the scene complete.

Cassie's Christmas Palace
By René Lackey

Cassie stared at the classroom clock. How could she break the news to her sister, Jenna? Mom wasn't coming home, so there wouldn't be any joy to share on Christmas Day.

"Attention, Crestview High students and faculty." The principal's voice came through the loud speakers. "Whether you've been naughty or nice, I wish you a Merry Christmas and Happy New Year. Don't forget to drop off your donations as you leave."

The dismissal bell sounded, and everyone bolted for the door. Except for Cassie, who trailed behind because she had no donation to leave.

With quick steps onto the bus, Cassie escaped the cold north wind but not the chill that made her hands tremble when she wiped the frost from the window. How could she tell Jenna about Mom's phone call last night?

"Cassie, I'm in jail," Mom had said. "I'll explain later. Please don't call your grandmother. You know what she'll do. There's fifty dollars under my mattress.